Pissarro

p.172

Pissarro

Curator
Guillermo Solana

Museo Thyssen-Bornemisza, Madrid
June 4, 2013 – September 15, 2013

Obra Social "la Caixa", CaixaForum, Barcelona
October 15, 2013 – January 26, 2014

Lenders

Belgium

Liège   BAL – Musée des Beaux-Arts
de Liège

Canada

Montreal   The Montreal Museum of Fine Arts
Ottawa   National Gallery of Canada

Denmark

Copenhagen   Ordrupgaard

France

Douai   Musée de la Chartreuse
Grenoble   Musée de Grenoble
Le Havre   MuMa – Musée d'art moderne
André Malraux
Paris   Musée d'Orsay
Musée Marmottan Monet
Petit Palais Musée des
Beaux-Arts de la Ville de Paris
Toulouse   Fondation Bemberg
Valenciennes   Musée des Beaux-Arts de
Valenciennes

Germany

Essen   Museum Folkwang
Hamburg   Hamburger Kunsthalle
Hannover   Niedersächsisches
Landesmuseum
Karlsruhe   Staatliche Kunsthalle
Wuppertal   Von der Heydt-Museum

Hungary

Budapest   Szépmüvészeti Múzeum

Italy

Florence   Galleria d'arte moderna di
Palazzo Pitti

Mexico

Mexico City   Pérez Simón Collection

Netherlands

Amsterdam   Van Gogh Museum
Rotterdam   Museum Boijmans van Beuningen

Spain

Madrid   Carmen Thyssen-Bornemisza
Collection, on deposit at the
Museo Thyssen-Bornemisza
Museo Thyssen-Bornemisza

Switzerland

Basel   Kunstmuseum Basel
La Chaux-De-Fonds   Musée des beaux-arts
Lugano   Museo Cantonale d'Arte
Neuchâtel   Musée d'art et d'histoire

United Kingdom

Birmingham   The Barber Institute of Fine Arts,
University of Birmingham
Cardiff   National Museum Wales
Glasgow   Glasgow Museums
Ipswich   Colchester & Ipswich Museums
London   Tate
The National Gallery
Manchester   Manchester Art Galleries
Oxford   The Ashmolean Museum
Southampton   Southampton City Art Gallery

United States

Atlanta   High Museum of Art
Birmingham   Birmingham Museum of Art
Brooklyn   Brooklyn Museum
Buffalo   Albright-Knox Art Gallery
Chicago   The Art Institute of Chicago
Columbus   Columbus Museum of Art
Denver   Denver Art Museum
Philadelphia   Philadelphia Museum of Art
Fort Worth   Kimbell Art Museum
Los Angeles   Hammer Museum
Memphis   Memphis Brooks Museum of Art
Muskegon   Muskegon Museum of Art
New Haven   Yale University Art Gallery
New Orleans   New Orleans Museum of Art
New York   The Metropolitan Museum of Art
Norfolk   Chrysler Museum of Art
Phoenix   Phoenix Art Museum
Washington   Corcoran Gallery of Art
National Gallery of Art
Williamstown   Sterling and Francine Clark
Art institute
Williams College Museum of Art

Spanish Ministry of Education, Culture, and Sport

The exhibition opening at the Museo Thyssen-Bornemisza this summer – and traveling to CaixaForum Barcelona this fall – offers visitors the opportunity to contemplate, for the first time in Spain, a retrospective of the work of Camille Pissarro, the only painter who participated in the eight exhibitions of the impressionist group organized in Paris between 1874 and 1886.

Curated by Guillermo Solana, Artistic Director of the Museo Thyssen-Bornemisza, the show features a selection of seventy-nine works that offer a chronological vision of Pissarro's artistic development from his arrival in France from his native Saint Thomas in 1855 up to his death in 1903.

A champion of anarchist ideas, Pissarro believed in the possibility of creating an artists' cooperative, and although this project never materialized, his generosity and sense of collective purpose led him to become a mentor, master, and friend to fellow artists such as Monet, Renoir, Sisley, Degas, Cézanne, Gauguin, Seurat, Signac, Caillebotte, and Guillaumin, among others.

While the most frequently recurring subjects in Pissarro's work are landscapes and rural scenes – specifically of the outskirts of Paris, the areas around Louveciennes and, especially, Pontoise and Eragny, where he resided for long periods and executed most of his *plein air* work – this exhibition also presents the urban views that, owing to his delicate health during the last ten years of his life, he produced from the windows of his studios in Paris, Rouen, Dieppe, and Le Havre.

Pissarro has been made possible thanks to the collaboration of numerous institutions and private collections that have generously loaned works to the exhibition. We take this opportunity to express our most sincere gratitude to them all.

Guillermo Solana

Artistic Director, Museo Thyssen-Bornemisza

"Humble and colossal," as his friend Cézanne described him, Camille Pissarro is perhaps the most important figure of impressionism and at the same time the least familiar of the movement's members. It was Pissarro who in 1873 drafted the statutes of the artists' cooperative that launched the exhibitions of the impressionist group, and he was the only painter who participated in all eight of those shows, from 1874 to 1886. And yet, despite this, Pissarro's career was eclipsed by the immense success of his friend Claude Monet.

The Museo Thyssen-Bornemisza has two canvases by Pissarro in its permanent holdings and four others on loan from the Carmen Thyssen Collection. For this reason, we believed it was only right for the Museum to present the first retrospective of the artist ever held in Spain. The exhibition focuses on his landscape painting, the genre that overwhelmingly predominates in Pissarro's oeuvre. It is organized chronologically, according to the places where the painter resided and worked. Pissarro spent most of his life in towns such as Louveciennes, Pontoise, and Eragny, but the last two rooms of the show are devoted to the urban landscapes he painted during the last decade of his life: his views of Paris and London, Rouen, Dieppe, and Le Havre.

I would like to express my profound gratitude to the museums and collectors from around the world who have generously helped make this exhibition possible through the loan of works. Likewise, I should like to acknowledge the two foremost scholars of Pissarro's work, Richard R. Brettel and Joachim Pissarro, for their inestimable contribution to this catalogue. Finally, I want to thank the entire team at the Museo Thyssen-Bornemisza and in particular the technical curator, Paula Luengo, for her enthusiastic and impeccable work.

English Channel

Berneval-le-Grand
Dieppe
Varengeville-sur-Mer

Le Havre

Rouen

Epte

Seine

Bazincourt   Eragny-sur-Epte

Oise

Giverny   La Roche-Guyon   Osny   Auvers

Pontoise   Saint-Ouen-l'Aumône

Montmorency

Marne

Marly-le-Roi   Paris

Louveciennes   Passy   Saint-Maur

Bougival

Versailles   La Varenne-Saint-Hilaire

Seine

Barbizon

Fontainebleau   Seine

Moret-sur-Loing

Yonne

Loing

Contents

pp. 12–13
Camille Pissarro
The Orchard at Eragny, 1896
[cat. 52 detail]

Note
Throughout this volume, the reader will find the abbreviation PDR and a number in brackets following the titles of Pissarro's works. This number refers to the work's designation in the catalogue raisonné by Joachim Pissarro and Claire Durand-Ruel Snollaerts, *Pissarro: Critical Catalogue of Paintings / Pissarro: Catalogue critique des peintures*, 3 vols. (Paris: Wildenstein Institute; Milan: Skira, 2005).

Guillermo Solana

The Road in Pissarro

Guillermo Solana

The Road in Pissarro

If one were to choose a single visual subject that sums up Pissarro's entire oeuvre, that subject could well be *the road*: a street leading out of a town, a track cutting through a field, a path meandering into a wood. At times, the road coincides with the vanishing lines of a composition; at others, it follows the curve bordering a vegetable garden or the skirt of a hillside – motifs that multiply the representational possibilities. In his late Paris canvases, the artist focused on perspective views of the city's main arteries, such as the Avenue de l'Opéra or the Boulevard Montmartre. The difficulty of the road subject in Pissarro's oeuvre lies in its ubiquity. How can one characterize an element that appears everywhere, and from the most variegated points of view?

The most obvious function of the road is to give the viewer access to the pictorial space and to measure its depth, going as far, perhaps, as the horizon itself. But its mission is not always so simple. At times the covert purpose of the road consists in slowing the advance of the viewer's gaze; hence the zigzags, meanders or interruptions (like the road that disappears behind a hill and reappears on the other side), which serve to delay the eye's progress towards the horizon, obliging it to pause and explore the landscape.

Every road links space and time together, producing narrative meaning. In the paintings of the classical masters, the road provided a stage for such subjects as the Flight into Egypt, the Way of the Cross or the Road to Emmaus. The Romantics retained the sacred aura of the road in the figure of the pilgrim, but they also made it into a space of errant wandering for artists, itinerant peddlers and vagabonds. This is the case with as late a figure as Courbet, for example, whose scenes always develop on a road or near it. Though Pissarro, like other impressionists, seems to have eschewed narrative in his paintings, in his work the road – even when devoid of human figures – nevertheless remains profoundly allusive, deeply evocative.

Front and profile

In an essay on seventeenth-century Dutch painting, Paul Claudel draws attention to the apparently banal distinction between landscapes seen "in profile" and those presented "from the front":

Up to now I have spoken of that class of landscapes presented to us, if I may say so, by the slice and as if in profile. There is quite another kind of which Hobbema's *Avenue of Trees* is typical, or the paintings of Van der Neer, of which we get a full view. There is a road, a canal, a more or less winding stream that opens before us an imaginary expanse at the center, and invites us to explore it. Or sometimes beyond the darkened, detailed foreground, which is cut out like a silhouette, there is a luminous curtain that separates reality from desire, and beyond which appears a distant city, a faraway town. We are introduced, I was about to say breathed in, to the interior of the composition, and for us reverie is transformed into charm. Where are we?[1]

Let us consider two of Pissarro's paintings from the mid-1860s, when the artist had settled with his family in Pontoise. In the first of these, *The House of Père Gallien, Pontoise* [cat. 5], a man and a woman stroll along a path beneath a fruit tree in bloom (the tree seems to be planted in the middle of this path). Two village women appear in the distance. Are the elegantly dressed couple two visitors from the city, or are they members of the local bourgeoisie? In the other painting, *Banks of the Oise at Pontoise* [cat. 6], there is also a man and a woman, but the lack of an apparent relationship between them eliminates any sense of anecdote from the work. The man gazes up at the large chimney, drawing our attention to it. The smokestack, belonging to the recently opened gasworks, occupies the same place in this painting as the tree in the other work. As if to accentuate the industrial aspect, another small smokestack appears alongside the first and, in the distance, the iron railway bridge built in 1863 that connected Pontoise to Paris.

Richard R. Brettell was the first to underscore the dual character of Pontoise in Pissarro's work, with its combination of rural and urban aspects. "It is customary," Brettell observes, "to consider Pissarro as a painter of 'la vie agreste' [...] Pissarro's views of the city of Pontoise, painted in 1867 and 1868, make it clear that he embraced rather than ignored the industrial character of Pontoise.[2] In this light, it is not far-fetched to consider the two paintings discussed here as representing two antithetical facets of Pontoise: *the old rural idyll*, on the one hand, and *the new, industrial progress* on the other. Now then, are these differences not reflected in the very arrangement of the road in each work? The path in the painting of the couple under the tree crosses the image, while in the second canvas, it is at a much sharper angle to the picture plane, reinforced by the row of trees on the right. The dominant horizontal, on the one hand, suggests the absence of tension, stagnation even, while the road tending toward the perpendicular seems to indicate an active impulse and an orientation towards the future.

In early 1869, Pissarro left Pontoise for Louveciennes, a town with a thousand inhabitants on the banks of the Seine. There he rented a large house on one of the main roads, which led to Versailles. Pissarro's colleagues gradually ended up visiting the area. In the summer of 1869, Monet and Renoir painted in nearby Bougival, and in December Monet moved to Louveciennes. In their Louveciennes landscapes, Pissarro and Monet would experiment together with perspectives of the Route de Versailles, varying the angle with the picture plane and the width of the visual field [fig. 2 and cat. 8]. Their views of the tree-lined road in winter have the sobriety and theatrical power of Hobbema's celebrated painting, *The Avenue at Middelharnis* [fig. 1].[3] Like Hobbema, Pissarro and Monet used the trees to control the regular rhythm of the receding space, which otherwise might have seemed almost vertiginous, as is the case with the approaches to perspective of Caillebotte, Van Gogh or Munch. Monet and Pissarro, however, add an element that is barely evident in Hobbema: shadows.

Joachim Pissarro has emphasized the importance of two aspects intertwined in a dialogic relationship in Pissarro's Louveciennes landscapes, namely, shadow and structure.[4] The buildings, the trees and the road are the material supports for the space and they make up its fundamental structure; the shadows, meanwhile, create a secondary, ghostly structure. Thus, for example, in Monet's painting, *Road, Winter Effect, Sunset* [fig. 2], the shadows from the trees on the left repeat the shape of the road in perspective, like an echo. Pissarro employs analogous devices in *Route de Versailles, Louveciennes, Winter Sun and Snow* [cat. 8], in which the variously sized trees along the road stand unaligned in different positions, as if oblivious to their function in creating the illusion of perspective. Rather, it is the shadows, cast rhythmically in oblique lines across the road, which assume this role. This emancipation of the shadow earned Pissarro reproach from the critic Castagnary: "He commits the grave error of painting on the ground (*Gelée blanche*) the shadows cast by the trees situated outside the frame, and which the viewer must assume exist, since they are not visible [...].

Fig. 1
Meindert Hobbema
The Avenue at Middelharnis, 1689
Oil on canvas, 103.5 × 141 cm
The National Gallery, London,
purchased 1871, NG830

Fig. 2
Claude Monet
Road, Winter Effect, Sunset, 1869
Oil on canvas, 42 × 64 cm
Musée d'Orsay, on loan to the Musées
des Beaux-Arts de Rouen, Rouen

Camille Pissarro
Route de Versailles, Louveciennes,
Winter Sun and Snow, c. 1870
[cat. 8]

Fig. 3
Camille Pissarro
Lordship Lane Station, Dulwich, 1871
Oil on canvas, 44.5 × 72.5 cm
The Courtauld Gallery, London,
P.1948.SC.317

Fig. 4
Camille Pissarro
Crystal Palace, 1871
Oil on canvas, 47.2 × 73.5 cm
The Art Institute of Chicago, gift of
Mr. and Mrs. B. E. Bensinger, 1972.1164

Camille Pissarro
Near Sydenham Hill, 1871
[cat. 10]

Camille Pissarro
Dulwich College, c. 1871
[cat. 11]

But these flaws in logic or lack of good taste do not diminish the lovely qualities of his skilful execution."[5]

Let us now return to the distinction between views "from the front" and views "in profile." During the brief but decisive period Pissarro spent in London between December 1870 and June 1871, the artist confronted a scenario even more sharply marked by the rural-industrial divide than was the case in Pontoise. Industrialization is the dominant subject of a painting like *Lordship Lane Station, Dulwich* [fig. 3], one of the first appearances of the train in impressionist painting, inspired in Turner's work from 1844, *Rain, Steam and Speed*, which Pissarro saw in London and which especially intrigued him.[6] To express the impact of progress, Pissarro presents the locomotive heading directly towards the viewer, as if it were severing the landscape in two. In *Crystal Palace* [fig. 4], he also applies a decidedly central perspective. The wall and the short houses on the right lead the foot traffic and our gaze towards the Crystal Palace, which in its transparent immateriality, as if constructed out of light and air, stands as a symbol of a radiant future. Pissarro thus adopts a frontal perspective in the two most emblematic images of industrial progress he painted in England, organized around a road that penetrates the center of the painting.

In other London works, in contrast, he adopts an oblique composition. Such is the case of *Near Sydenham Hill* [cat. 10], where the train is no longer a threatening machine heading towards the viewer but a trace of smoke in the background. To distance it even more, it is framed by the horizontal path and three trees, which stand like the columns of a classical portico. Another painting, *Dulwich College* [cat. 11], presents a nearly identical diagonal composition between two vertical supports on the right and the left. These paintings, in which the road crosses the picture plane, stand at a remove from the world of industrialization, seeking refuge in nostalgic pastorals.

One could be tempted to follow this apparent association – between transverse road and rural idyll, on the one hand, and the road viewed frontally and industrial progress, on the other – in Pissarro's work subsequent to his time in London. This assumption is quickly belied, however. In 1873, Pissarro devoted an important series of paintings to the factory in Saint-Ouen-l'Aumône, situated across from Pontoise on the other side of the river [see cat. 6 and fig. 27]. In the paintings from this series, the chimneys and industrial buildings are approached successively from different points of view and

represented on various occasions in compositions based on the most stable sort of horizontality, which lends them a classical air.

Moving forward, into the open

Back in France, Pissarro continued to explore the possibilities offered by the frontal depiction of the road. In representing the *Rue des Voisins* [cat. 12] in Louveciennes, a setting revisited also by Renoir and Sisley (who painted it after a snowfall), Pissarro omits any sort of distraction on the sides (for instance, the entrance to the Château des Voisins, which is on the left) so as to concentrate on the street "squeezed in" between the houses in the town. In his painting of a park lane at the Château de Marly [cat. 13], the little wood completely envelops the path and accentuates the sense of a corridor, almost like a tunnel. In both cases, the penetrating effect of the central perspective is intensified by the downward slope, which accelerates our inward journey into the painting.

The road presented frontally, however, also offers the opposite possibility, that of moving forward, into the open. It is true that in Pissarro's oeuvre, large, open expanses are rare. As Brettell has pointed out, in Pontoise land was divided into small fields and orchards, and this division produced a "concentrated landscape" that Pissarro found particularly captivating. In this countryside, architecture and vegetation are interwoven; one's gaze pauses on trees and rooftops, and fences and walls direct its movement within the image. The prevalent sensation is one of proximity and tactility. In contrast, representations of extensive fields of grain are very limited in Pissarro's output[7]. Yet they do exist: a first example would be the series *The Four Seasons* (1872–73), commissioned by Achille Arosa, of which two paintings, *Summer* [fig. 5] and *Autumn*, are panoramic landscapes of fields of grain. In the vast plains, our gaze tends to wander aimlessly, but the road provides a focus that guides it. The same organizing concept appears in *June Morning, View over the Hills of Pontoise* [fig. 6], where the narrowing effect of the road executed in perspective adds a certain dramatic intensity to the work.

It might be useful here to contrast the view "from the front" and "in profile" of Pissarro's large, open spaces. In *Road to Ennery* [cat. 17] in Pontoise, some villagers move along the

Fig. 5
Camille Pissarro
Summer, 1872
Oil on canvas, 55 × 130 cm
Private collection

Fig. 6
Camille Pissarro
June Morning, View over the Hills of Pontoise, 1873
Oil on canvas, 54 × 91 cm
Staatliche Kunsthalle, Karlsruhe, 2539

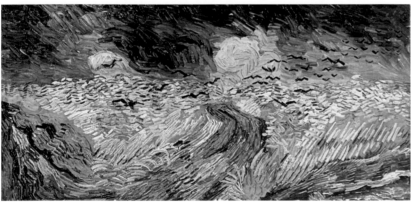

Camille Pissarro
*The Old Road to Ennery at
Pontoise*, 1877
[cat. 30]

Fig. 7
Vincent van Gogh
Wheatfield with Crows, 1890
Oil on canvas, 50.5 × 103 cm
Van Gogh Museum, Amsterdam, F779

road that is laid out parallel to the picture plane and to the horizon. The viewer lacks an imaginary point of entry into the landscape, which can only be contemplated from outside, as if it were a closed world. All of the emphasis falls on the flat geometry of the image, in the fields divided into triangles and trapezoids. One of the principal lines climbs on the right towards the horizon: it is the highway leading from Pontoise to the nearby village of Ennery, and it will be the subject of the following painting.

The Old Road to Ennery at Pontoise [cat. 30] is a deceptively simple painting with certain lurking ambiguities. The dominant road represented frontally ends at an intersecting lane that traverses the entire painting. It seems to present a flat stretch of land, but it soon becomes clear that the ground slopes downwards on the right. The central road, in its twists and turns, anticipates Van Gogh's turbulent *Wheatfield with Crows* [fig. 7] – with the noteworthy difference that around the central road, Pissarro includes a series of marks in the ground that converge and point towards the horizon, while in Van Gogh's, the roads fork out and diverge, none of them leading towards the horizon, for they either end blindly or veer off the sides of the painting.

The art of (im)balance

In the landscapes we have seen up to this point, the road is either perpendicular or parallel to the picture plane. In both cases, an orthogonal matrix dominates the composition. This arrangement, however, is not the only possibility in Pissarro's work. In his preliminary study to the catalogue raisonné of the painter's oeuvre, Joachim Pissarro establishes a fundamental distinction between the artist's two compositional methods, "one based on right angles, the other, which Cézanne was equally adept in, teasingly askew":

When using the orthogonal method, Pissarro builds up the pictorial space with a system of lines that intersect perpendicularly for the most part, creating the impression that the picture surface is given over to a well-constructed aggregate of vertical and horizontal planes (stone walls, ploughed fields with essentially horizontal or vertical striations). When using the imbalanced composition, on the other hand, he places the viewer in the position of someone perched with one foot on solid ground

and the other on a sloping plane or overhang. The latter is a
strange method, with the perspective appearing to fall away to
the left or to the right under the artist's feet, at once fascinating
and oddly disorienting. It structures some of the most absorbing
works of Pissarro's impressionist period: the Brooklyn Museum's
The Climb, Rue de la Côte-du-Jalet, Pontoise [cat. 18] is one
noteworthy example; so is *Houses at L'Hermitage, Pontoise*
[fig. 10], and there is a host of analogous compositions. Pissarro,
Cézanne and Gauguin (especially in some of the latter's Brittany
landscapes) were the only artists to push this technique to the
point where it actually inspires one with a feeling of dizziness.
All three of them were fascinated by highly unusual compositions
that seem to undermine the very position of the artist, as if to
emphasize how eminently precarious his point of view really is.[8]

Camille Pissarro
Chemin des Creux, Louvecienes, Snow, 1872
[cat. 14]

The fundamental importance of this passage lies in its
unveiling the fact that *The Climb*, a painting whose striking
originality has always been stressed, is not an island but
rather the apex of a *submerged continent* in Pissarro's oeuvre
– and that in Pissarro one may find the seed not only of the
constructive character of the painting of Cézanne and that
of the early Gauguin, but also their *de-constructive* aspects.
Particularly acute is Joachim Pissarro's observation that
the painter's experiments (as well as those of his disciples,
Cézanne and Gauguin) can produce "a feeling of dizziness."
Could the wise, temperate Pissarro have thus been a master
of vertigo?

The "imbalanced composition" finds early precedents in the
artist's oeuvre. For example, Pissarro's landscape *Banks of
the Marne* [cat. 4], despite his classicizing intentions, suggests
an unstable equilibrium produced by the slope on one side,
not unlike the painting by Corot that probably inspired it,
Le Petit Chaville, near Ville-d'Avray, c. 1823 [fig. 8]. Another
example is the magnificent *Chemin des Creux, Louveciennes,
Snow* [cat. 14], in which the road, nearly obliterated under
the snow, is furthermore juxtaposed with rough terrain marked
by sharp differences in height.

This is even clearer in two of his paintings of the Ruelle des
Poulies, in Pontoise, from 1872. In the first of these paintings
[fig. 9], the path leads from the foreground towards a cluster
of nearby houses, while on the right a bell tower and other
buildings seem to emerge mysteriously out of the ground. The
second painting [cat. 16] of the same place solves the mystery
and at the same time flips the precarious imbalance of the

Fig. 8
Jean-Baptiste-Camille Corot
Le Petit Chaville, near Ville-d'Avray, c. 1823
Oil on canvas, 24.8 × 34 cm
The Ashmolean Museum, Oxford, A642

Camille Pissarro
Banks of the Marne, 1864
[cat. 4]

Fig. 9
Camille Pissarro
Le Palais de Justice, Pontoise, 1872
Oil on canvas, 40.5 × 54.5 cm
Musée d'Orsay, Paris, RF 1683

Camille Pissarro
Ruelle des Poulies at Pontoise, c. 1872
[cat. 16]

Camille Pissarro
*The Climb, Rue de la
Côte-du-Jalet, Pontoise*, 1875
[cat. 18]

Camille Pissarro
*The Côte des Boeufs
at L'Hermitage*, 1877
[cat. 23]

composition. The point of view has been shifted to the right and now falls directly on the slope of the hill. Below, on the right, the buildings of the town appear, among them the bell tower and the smokestack of the gasworks.[9] It is as if a great hollow had been carved out, and the road with its eccentric curve had been left above, skirting the small abyss.

The painting already alluded to titled *The Climb* constitutes a more radical step in this exploration of (im)balance. The basic elements of the composition, the road on the hillside and the view of a hamlet in the distance had already been employed by Pissarro in the landscapes he painted at the Hermitage in the 1860s. Here they reappear, however, in an extraordinarily novel arrangement. This road up a hillside seems almost outrageously eccentric. Held up by rocks that jut out, the path seems to climb like a catwalk hanging over a void. It places us at the edge of a ravine, with one foot on the ground and the other in the air. For a moment we have the sense that the path continues downhill but realize that it is a stone wall. As for the trees and bushes, which in the play of light and shadow disguise the space, it is difficult to decide whether they contribute to the sense of confusion or provide some kind of protection against the feeling of vertigo. Looking up, the traveler spies the familiar houses of the Hermitage through a convenient opening in the foliage.

A screen of trees

The Climb is intimately linked to another important canvas painted on the hills of Pontoise, *The Côte des Boeufs at L'Hermitage* [cat. 23]. In *The Climb*, the path off to one side and the screen of trees play complementary roles in provoking the viewer's disorientation. In *The Côte des Boeufs*, the only visible part of the path is a small curve in the proscenium, on the left, which leaves the frame almost as soon as it has entered it. (We intuit another segment of the path, where the two peasant women appear, as if lying in ambush.) The screen of trees, a common device in Pissarro, has hypertrophied to the point that it covers the entire picture surface. Lionello Venturi explains it in the following terms: "The motive is clear: in order to obtain the fusion of objects and atmosphere, the painter seeks the continual interruption of the visible elements. The lights and shadows pursue each other so closely that they create a unique vibration."[10] The screen, however, can serve other functions. The horizon of *The Côte des Boeufs* presents a steep incline, and the parallel tree trunks, like iron bars, seem designed to contain the high ground, compensating for the imbalance.

In the mid 1870s, Pissarro created further "unstable" paths in other landscapes presenting steep slopes or terraces, such as *Houses at L'Hermitage, Pontoise* [fig. 10] and *View of the Mathurin House, Pontoise* [fig. 11], both from 1875. As Joachim Pissarro has pointed out, Cézanne would become the great, enthusiastic heir to Pissarro in the creation of complex compositions such as these, touched by a magical (im)balance. Gauguin would not follow far behind. At the same time that Pissarro painted – again – a road going uphill in Osny [cat. 37], Gauguin worked alongside him at the same spot and created a strange, unreal composition, whose effect is remarkably flat: *Landscape from Osny*, 1883 [fig. 12].

Connections between Pissarro's art of (im)balance can also be made with other impressionist painters besides Cézanne and Gauguin. The art dealer René Gimpel once quoted Degas's impertinent remark to Monet regarding an exhibition of his water lilies at Durand-Ruel's gallery in 1909: "I was at your exhibition for only a second, your paintings gave me vertigo."[11] The complaint sounds paradoxical coming from the painter of *Miss La La at the Cirque Fernando* or of the Museo Thyssen-Bornemisza's *Dancer in Green*. It would not be far-fetched to draw a parallel between Pissarro's compositional experiments in the hills of L'Hermitage and the unusual points of view that Degas adopts in his scenes from the Paris Opera, exploiting the differences in height between the theatre boxes, the stage and the orchestra pit.

Enclosed fields

When he moved first to Osny and shortly thereafter to Eragny, Pissarro lost that mixture of the rural and the urban that was a peculiarity of Pontoise. As if to compensate for the loss, he showed a new interest in large cities. The painter's first productive period in Rouen, a starting point for his urban series, dates from 1883, the same year he was settling in at Eragny. Throughout the 1890s, Pissarro's sojourns in Eragny alternated with long visits to major cities and, alongside his rural landscapes, he began to create a growing number of paintings devoted to Paris, London and Rouen.

Fig. 10
Camille Pissarro
Houses at L'Hermitage, Pontoise, 1875
Oil on canvas, 61 × 71 cm
Private collection

Fig. 11
Camille Pissarro
View of the Mathurin House, Pontoise, 1875
Oil on canvas, 52 × 81 cm
Private collection

Camille Pissarro
Sente de la Ravinière, Osny, 1883
[cat. 37]

Fig. 12
Paul Gauguin
Landscape from Osny, 1883
Oil on canvas, 76.5 × 101 cm
Ny Carlsberg Glyptotek, Copenhagen

As Joachim Pissarro reminds us, the numerous landscapes produced in Eragny correspond to "a few acres of the fields and trees expanding in front of his window."[12] From the outset of his career, Pissarro had painted enclosed fields. Starting in 1884–85, the walled garden or meadow became the almost exclusive subject of his rural landscapes. The painter frequently introduced the figure of a peasant woman as the protagonist of these nearby familiar domestic spaces. When there is no human figure, a tree stands in its place: a tree represented with its individual features, portrayed as if it was a character. Such is the case with the Great Walnut tree – *Grand Noyer* – that appears with such frequency in the landscapes from Eragny [cat. 48] and with the small apple tree with its twisted trunk [cat. 49], alongside other generic trees: pears, plums, poplars, etc.

And what of the roads? Pissarro still painted them at the beginning of his period at Eragny, but starting in 1885 we rarely encounter them in his rural landscapes. One might say that something had made the very idea of a road impossible or superfluous. In the reiterated images of the area around Eragny, time appears to have stood still.

But roads do not disappear from Pissarro's work. They simply move to the city and take on a new existence, reincarnated in the park lanes of London, in the avenues and boulevards of Paris, and in the bridges of Rouen.

Urban vertigo

Around 1890, most of the original members of the impressionist group had left Paris, and the one painter who up to that point had devoted all of his efforts to portraying the life of the countryside would be the one to take on the task of painting the capital. The last decade of Pissarro's oeuvre is dominated by his travels to London, Rouen, Dieppe and Paris. Out of these travels emerged various series, undoubtedly related to Monet's work but also distinct from that painter's approach, as Joachim Pissarro reveals in the present catalogue.

Although Pissarro never explained his devotion to cities in writing, his correspondence can serve to illuminate his ideas about the matter – for example, in the passage in which he ponders on the specific character of modern beauty and provides an ironic example with the Eiffel Tower (represented in the first drawing in the series *Turpitudes Sociales*):

Much may be said of the search for modern beauty, for the beautiful in general. What could it be in our humbug (joke) era? Could it be the beauty of the Greeks? That cold, pagan, measured beauty seems to lie outside our philosophical beliefs. Could it be Japanese, Chinese or Indian beauty? Think of our way of life, our dress, and you will see that the tendency of their philosophical and religious ideas does not correspond to our temperament. What then? The Eiffel Tower? It is terrifying. Ah, yes, that is modern beauty! So my first drawing in this series shows you the philosopher contemplating with irony the tower that strives to conceal the rising star and the new ideal![13]

Pissarro's work in Paris, however, did not arise in response to a theoretical proposition, but rather as a result of a physical ailment: "I will probably leave for Eragny tomorrow. I feel much better, but I will have to keep my eye bandaged for another eight days. I shall try to work with one eye; Degas does it and gets good results; he has only one good eye!"[14] At that point Pissarro did not attempt to paint in Paris yet; his first period working in the capital city would begin two years later. In February 1893, when the painter was compelled to remain in Paris for an extended length of time in order to treat an abscess in his eye, Pissarro's doctor recommended that he avoid the dusty streets of the city, so he shut himself away in his room in the Hôtel de Rome, from whose windows he could paint the Rue Saint-Lazare, the Place du Havre, the Rue d'Amsterdam and the Gare Saint-Lazare. This biographical anecdote is not lacking in unintentional irony. The fact that it all began because of an eye disease is a curious coincidence, if one recalls that impressionism was *diagnosed* by its critics as an impairment of vision. Pissarro himself disputed with Huysmans over the matter.[15] It also strikes one as paradoxical that the landscape painter should retreat from the countryside in order to recover his health in the great metropolis...

Pissarro's eye problems forced him to work regularly indoors. When a certain amateur offered him a spot near Rouen with a splendid view of the city, Pissarro declined with ironic resignation, "but I am not thirty years old now, I have to be satisfied with a hotel window."[16] Throughout the 1890s, the majority of Pissarro's landscapes – whether rural, from Eragny, or urban, from Rouen, Dieppe, Le Havre or Paris – were painted from a window.

The most lucid response to Pissarro's first views of Paris, exhibited in 1894 at the Durand-Ruel gallery, are a few brief lines from the critic Paul Dupray: "In the Parisian physiognomies (*Cour du Havre – Place Saint-Lazare*), the viewer will find vignettes expressing life in the streets with a keen intelligence of the urban hustle and bustle."[17] That *vertige urbain* could refer to the quick tempo of life in Paris, which Pissarro captures so well in the streets teeming with figures and carriages. But this vertigo is also, more literally, the sensation that is created when the artist, who had formerly worked with his feet firmly planted on the ground, looks down from a window, painting high-angle views of the streets of Paris.

Pissarro thus advanced deep into a territory explored earlier by Monet in his views of the Boulevard des Capucines [see fig. 16] and then by Caillebotte in his extraordinary boulevards. In his now classic text on aerial views in the modern art tradition, Kirk Varnedoe situates Pissarro's Parisian series in the wake of Caillebotte's experiments. Like Caillebotte, Pissarro ended up eliminating the horizon in some of these works, such that they produce forms which appear to float within the visual field. The high-angle point of view cancels out the conventional signs of anisotropy, that is, the directional sense of up and down, the value of the force of gravity. The street becomes a collection of forms randomly distributed on a plane. For Varnedoe, these aerial views, subsequently developed further in avant-garde photography by Rodchenko, Moholy-Nagy, André Kertész and many others, anticipated the vertiginous all-over of Jackson Pollock's painting.[18]

Multitudes

I am returning to Paris again on the tenth, to do a series of the boulevard des Italiens. Last time I did several small canvases – about 13 × 10 inches – of the rue Saint-Lazare, effects of rain, snow, etc., with which Durand was very pleased. A series of paintings of the boulevards seems to him a good idea, and it will be interesting to overcome the difficulties. I engaged a large room at the Grand Hôtel de Russie, 1 rue Drouot, from which I can see the whole sweep of boulevards almost as far as the Porte Saint-Denis, anyway as far as the boulevard Bonne-Nouvelle.[19]

Looking out the window of that room, in February 1897 Pissarro began a series – the most systematic one he had ever undertaken – devoted to the Boulevard Montmartre

[cats. 63 and 64]. The thirteen canvases that make up the series share the same point of view and framing, but differ in terms of the season, the time of day, the condition of the sky, and, accordingly, the light, the foliage, and the density of traffic. The motif is like a monad in which the entire universe is reflected. The Boulevard Montmartre series represents a return to the road viewed in central perspective, as in Louveciennes, but with a tunnel effect owing to the so-called *rue-mur* (street-wall) that is a feature of Haussmann's Paris. According to this model, taken from the Rue de Rivoli and applied along the boulevards, each building ceases to be an autonomous entity, and the horizontal lines of its façade, with the decorative features of each floor, are extended along the façades of the adjacent buildings. The resulting continuity reinforces the depth of perspective.

In addition to the Boulevard Montmartre, from the window of his hotel Pissarro could discern, at a more forced angle, the Boulevard des Italiens, of which he painted two canvases: "To my left I have another motif, which is terribly difficult: almost as the crow flies, looking over the carriages, buses and people milling about between the large trees and big houses which I have to set up right – it's tricky [...]."[20] Here again there is a hint of urban vertigo. Its focus is to be found in the crowd below, which Pissarro plans to capture at its most fascinating moment. On February 13 he announces to his son, "I have unpacked and am stretching some large canvases. I am going to get one or two ready to paint the crowd on Shrove Tuesday. I don't know if I can manage it, I am very much afraid the serpentines will hamper me no end."[21] On Shrove Tuesday, around four in the afternoon, beneath a rain of streamers and confetti, the long parade of carriages and masked revelers passed below the painter's windows on the Boulevard Montmartre: "[...] I painted the boulevards with the crowds and the march of the Boeuf-Gras, with effects of sun on the serpentines and the trees, the crowd in the shadow."[22] Pissarro dedicated two different canvases to the subject [cat. 63].

Pissarro's boulevards delighted Durand-Ruel, who encouraged him to seek out a new Parisian subject. In mid-December of 1897, the painter finally found the ideal lookout:

I forgot to mention that I found a room in the Grand Hôtel du Louvre with a superb view of the Avenue de l'Opéra and the corner of the Place du Palais Royal! It is very beautiful to paint! Perhaps it is not aesthetic, but I am delighted to be able to paint these Paris streets that people have come to call ugly, but which are so silvery, so luminous and vital. They are so different from the boulevards. This is completely modern.[23]

Pissarro worked in the Hôtel du Louvre until April 26, 1898, and the fifteen paintings he produced deal with different aspects of the Place du Thêatre-Français, the Avenue de l'Opéra and the Rue Saint-Honoré [cats. 65 and 66]. Unlike the narrow perspectives of the Boulevard Montmartre, these new views are open and spacious.

In a review of Pissarro's exhibition at Durand-Ruel's gallery in 1898, Gustave Geffroy synthesized the image of the city that one comes away with from these representations:

Cities have a particular physiognomy: one that is transient, anonymous, busy, mysterious, which must tempt the artist [...] The air that we breathe is enclosed within these frames, conveying to us the emotion of our muddy streets, of our rain showers, of our avenues disappearing in a distant fog. In this authentic atmosphere, the mêlée of carriages and pedestrians swirls around, criss-crosses, and mingles, with a prodigious sense of the rhythmic movement of crowds. Time and again this social combat, visible in the restless comings and goings on the street, is captured and summed up by Pissarro, and one of the beauties of this series of canvases is the representation of the inescapable hustle and bustle of the living in the midst of this scenery on a given day.[24]

Camille Pissarro
Boulevard Montmartre,
Mardi Gras, 1897
[cat. 63]

The river is a road

The pendant to Baron Haussmann's modern Paris, with its bustling boulevards and avenues, is the port city spilling out onto the quays typified by Rouen, Le Havre and Dieppe. The first series of Rouen painted by Pissarro in 1883 is not an entirely urban one [cat. 77]. A rural air persists in it, and the clash between the old city and the new is not yet pronounced. In the views of the Cours de la Reine, the arrow of the cathedral appears in the distance alongside the factory smokestacks. There are also examples, however, of what would become the principal subject of his Rouen series: the bridges and the busiest stretch of the river. In his second visit to the city, from January to April of 1896, the painter stayed at the Grand Hôtel de Paris, situated between the Pont Boieldieu and the Pont Corneille, which allowed him to choose one

Camille Pissarro
Morning Sun in the Rue Saint-Honoré,
Place du Théâtre Français, 1898
[cat. 65]

Camille Pissarro
Rue Saint-Honoré in the Afternoon,
Effect of Rain, 1897
[cat. 66]

bridge or the other, looking either to the right or to the left [cats. 78 and 79]: "I wanted to render the animation of the hive that is the harbor of Rouen."[25] On successive return journeys to Rouen, in the autumn of 1896 and then in 1898, the river and its bridges, with their frenetic commercial and industrial activity [cats. 80 and 81], would continue to be at the center of Pissarro's interest, though from time to time he would paint splendid views of the cathedral and the old rooftops of the city [see fig. 17]. Pissarro's predominant interest in the modern life of the city did not stand in the way of his attention to its old nucleus, to whose protection he actively contributed, supporting the Society of Friends of the Monuments of Rouen with donations designed to help save the old city, which the town council had abandoned to its fate.

The bridges of Rouen invite a comparison with the views of the Chelsea and Charing Cross bridges that Pissarro had painted in 1890 [cat. 61]. Those London bridges – like the ones that Monet would represent beginning in 1899 – were contemplative visions, marked by an almost magical stillness in which the only possible movement is the vibration of the atmosphere. The bridges of Rouen, in contrast, are like the congested, palpitating arteries of a circulatory system: "with much traffic, carriages, pedestrians, workers on the quays, boats, smoke, mist in the distance, the whole scene fraught with animation and life."[26] Pissarro's interest in this urban landscape, however, is not sociological but genuinely aesthetic. In a letter to his son he ardently defends the peculiar beauty of the docks, so lacking in acceptability according to conventional standards:

> In the foreground, boats on the water, to the left of the station, the workers' quarters which extend along the quays up to

the iron bridge, the bridge Boieldieu, you should see all this in the morning when the light is misty and delicate. Well now, that fool Mourey is a vulgarian to think that such a scene is banal and commonplace. It is as beautiful as Venice, my dear, it has an extraordinary character and is really beautiful! It is art.[27]

A few weeks later he would dwell again on the aesthetic justification of the subjects he had chosen:

> I just dispatched to Eragny fifteen pictures, in which I tried to represent the movement, the life, the atmosphere of the harbor thronged with smoking ships, bridges, chimneys, sections of the city in the fog and mist, under the setting sun, etc. I think that what I have done is bolder than what I did last year. I had the luck to have boats with rose-colored, golden-yellow and black masts. One picture is colored like a Japanese print; that won't please the neo-catholics [...].[28]

The road is nearing its end. The bustling activity of the quays of Rouen would extend some kilometers downriver, to the port of Le Havre, to where Pissarro moved in 1903 to begin his last series of paintings [cat. 82], concluded in September, only a couple of months before his death. There, in the same busy locus of transit where he had alighted almost a half-century before from the steamship that had brought him from America, he wrote:

> My dear Georges, I have settled in at this hotel, next to the jetty. I see the big transatlantic steamers and other boats passing beneath my window all day long, from morning to night, with the docks, the traffic: it's splendid; I think I have a new series in mind which should be interesting.[29]

1. Paul Claudel, *The Eye Listens* (New York: Philosophical Press, 1950), p. 10.

2. Richard R. Brettell, "Camille Pissarro: A Revision," in *Camille Pissarro, 1830–1903* [exh. cat. Hayward Gallery, London, October 30, 1980 – January 11, 1981; Grand Palais, Paris, January 30 – April 27, 1981; Museum of Fine Arts, Boston, May 19 – August 9, 1981] (London: Arts Council of Great Britain; Boston, Museum of Fine Arts, 1980), p. 21.

3. It has been suggested that Pissarro could have seen Hobbema's painting at the National Gallery in London in May 1871. See Christopher Lloyd, "Camille Pissarro and Hans Holbein the Younger," *The Burlington Magazine* 117, no. 872 (November 1975): 722–26.

4. Joachim Pissarro, *Camille Pissarro* (New York: Abrams, 1993), pp. 66–69 (henceforward referred to as *Camille Pissarro*).

5. Jules Castagnary, "Exposition du boulevard des Capucines: Les Impressionnistes," *Le Siècle*, April 29, 1874, p. 3.

6. On February 20, 1883, in a letter to Lucien, Pissarro comments on Lucien's visit to the National Gallery with Esther, showing interest in only one artist, Turner: "You have seen the Turners, yet you don't mention them. Can it be that the famous painting *The Railway* [...] did not impress you?" Camille Pissarro, *Letters to his Son Lucien*, ed. John Rewald, trans. Lionel Abel (New York: Pantheon, 2nd ed., 1943), p. 22 (henceforward referred to as *Letters to his Son*).

7. "These landscapes exist as exceptional images within Pissarro's work. Their spaciousness, the spread of the land across the almost panoramic format is very unusual for Pissarro, who preferred less insistently rectangular formats and greater complexity or formal interaction." Richard R. Brettell, *Pissarro and Pontoise: The Painter in a Landscape* (New Haven: Yale University Press, 1990), pp. 58–60 (henceforward referred to as *Pissarro and Pontoise*).

8. Joachim Pissarro, "Camille Pissarro's Vision of History and Art," in Joachim Pissarro and Claire Durand-Ruel Snollaerts, *Pissarro: Critical Catalogue of Paintings*, 3 vols. (Paris: Wildenstein Institute; Milan: Skira, 2005), vol. 1, pp. 80–81 (henceforward referred to as *Critical Catalogue*).

9. Brettell has drawn attention to the diminished importance of the religious buildings in Pontoise in Pissarro's painting: "In Pissarro's Pontoise, Notre-Dame is no more important than the smokestack of the factory and less important than the rather common group of rural houses that dominate the foreground of the picture." *Pissarro and Pontoise*, pp. 49–50.

10. Lionello Venturi, *La via dell'impressionismo: da Manet a Cézanne* (Turin: Einaudi, 1970), p. 211.

11. René Gimpel, *Journal d'un collectionneur* (Paris: Calmann-Lévy, 1963), p. 179.

12. *Camille Pissarro*, p. 242.

13. Letter to Esther Isaacson, Eragny, December 29, 1889. *Correspondance de Camille Pissarro*, ed. Janine Bailly-Herzberg, 5 vols. [vol. 1: 1865–85; vol. 2: 1886–90; vol. 3: 1891–94; vol. 4: 1895–98; and vol. 5: 1899–1903] (Saint-Ouen-l'Aumône: Valhermeil, 1986–91), vol. 2, pp. 318–19 (henceforward referred to as *Correspondance*).

14. Letter to Lucien, Paris, January 13, 1891. *Letters to his Son*, p. 146.

15. See various letters to Lucien and to Huysmans, from May 9 to 15, 1883. In *Correspondance*, vol. 1, pp. 203–8.

16. Letter to Lucien, Rouen, January 23, 1896. *Letters to his Son*, p. 281.

17. Paul Dupray in *Le Journal des Artistes* (18 March 1894): 510. Quoted in *Critical Catalogue*, vol. 3, pp. 640–41.

18. "Overview: The Flight of the Mind," chapter 5 of *A Fine Disregard: What Makes Modern Art Modern*, by Kirk Varnedoe (London: Thames and Hudson, 1990), especially pp. 220–21.

19. Letter to Lucien, Eragny, February 8, 1897. *Letters to his Son*, p. 307.

20. Letter to Georges, Paris, February 13, 1897, quoted in Richard R. Brettell, *The Impressionist and the City: Pissarro's Series Paintings* (New Haven: Yale University Press, 1992), p. 59.

21. Letter to Lucien, Paris, February 13, 1897. *Letters to his Son*, p. 307.

22. Letter to Lucien, Paris, March 5, 1897. *Letters to his Son*, p. 308.

23. Letter to Lucien, Paris, December 15, 1897. *Letters to his Son*, p. 316.

24. Gustave Geffroy, *La Vie artistique*, 8 vols., Series 6 (Paris: E. Dentu, 1892–1903), vol. 6, 1900, pp. 183–85.

25. Letter to Lucien, Rouen, March 7, 1896. *Letters to his Son*, p. 283.

26. Letter to Lucien, Rouen, February 26, 1896. *Letters to his Son*, p. 283.

27. Letter to Lucien, Rouen, October 2, 1896. *Letters to his Son*, p. 297.

28. Letter to Lucien, Rouen, November 11, 1896. *Letters to his Son*, pp. 299–300.

29. Letter to Georges, Le Havre, July 11, 1903. *Correspondance*, vol. 5, pp. 357–58.

Joachim Pissarro

Monet / Pissarro in the 1890s: Serial Racing

Joachim Pissarro

Monet / Pissarro in the 1890s: Serial Racing

On November 9, 1903, shortly before his death, Pissarro received the last letter from someone he knew. The missive was signed by one of his oldest friends and impressionist colleagues: Claude Monet. Unfortunately, due to his fast deteriorating health and ensuing loss of consciousness, Pissarro was unable to read it. The document stated:

> Mon cher Pissarro,
>
> Je suis bien peiné de vous savoir malade, et j'espère qu'entouré de bons soins vous serez vite rétabli. Tant qu'à vos préoccupations au sujet de votre ancienne dette, vous n'avez pas à vous en soucier le moins du monde, vous savez bien qu'il y a beau temps que Durand-Ruel me l'a entièrement soldée. Soignez-vous donc sans vous tracasser et faites-moi donner de vos nouvelles.
>
> . . .
>
> A vous de tout cœur, et mes amitiés à tous les vôtres.
> Votre tout dévoué,
> Claude Monet[1]

Pissarro died four days later, on November 13, 1903.

Six weeks earlier, on September 29, Pissarro had attended the first anniversary of Zola's death (1840–1902) in Médan. Upon returning home, he developed a flu together with a bladder infection. This alarming situation went from bad to worse and soon developed into a full-blown sepsis that was poorly treated by a weak, non-invasive doctor. Pissarro did not recover.

But, what was this old debt to which Monet referred in his letter?

We know from the correspondence between Camille's wife, Julie Vellay, and their children that during the last days leading to his death, poor Pissarro suffered a great deal of pain and lost partial consciousness, eventually developing dementia. Among other symptoms, he became delirious and regularly bemoaned a problem that had long been resolved: the fact that his wife had borrowed a large sum of money from Monet while Pissarro had been in London in 1892. This loan was negotiated between Julie and Monet (without Pissarro's knowledge) in order to enable her to purchase the house where the Pissarro family – Camille, Julie, and their six children – had been living in Eragny for nearly a decade. When Pissarro heard about this, he was utterly shocked; the idea of borrowing money (and a large sum at that: 15,000 francs) from Monet was more than Pissarro could take. He never got

over it. Throughout his feverish and painful last few days, Pissarro relived that earlier traumatic experience: he simply could not bear (and had never accepted) the fact that his wife had contracted a debt with Monet to buy their house. This is what Monet's "*votre ancienne dette*"[2] referred to. This debt (as Monet explains) had long been settled by Paul Durand-Ruel, their shared art dealer who also acted as banker to all his artists. But it had not been settled in Pissarro's mind...

So, why would Pissarro (almost literally) lose his mind over this long resolved situation, more than a decade after the fact?

Pissarro was in London in 1892 when he received a letter from his wife informing him that she had decided to ask Monet for the sum needed to buy the house in Eragny (one and a half hours northwest of Paris) where the Pissarro family had been living since 1884, and which they had been leasing until then. Monet conceded to Julie's request, but demanded (politely, but firmly) in return that Julie let him have a painting he had already expressed a desire to own: *Peasant Women Planting Stakes*, 1891 [PDR 922]. To make things worse, Pissarro had just given this recently executed painting to his wife, who had previously refused to let Monet have it. Now Julie was faced with a dilemma: give in to Monet's request or let their house go. The fact that Julie accepted to give Monet a painting she had just received as a gift from her husband, while contracting a large debt (15,000 francs) with Monet behind Pissarro's back, was the source of a psychological shock from which the artist would never recover. For a measure of comparison, in 1895 Monet's *Cathedrals* were selling for around 12,000 French francs, while Pissarro's paintings were going for approximately a fifth of that amount.

What had led to this episode?

During the impressionist period – between 1874 (the first impressionist exhibition) and 1886 (the last impressionist exhibition) – Pissarro and Monet always kept close ties, but were not the best of friends. Pissarro felt more affinity towards Cézanne and Degas, and less towards Monet, Renoir and Sisley.

After 1886, however, Pissarro and Monet almost burned all bridges, as Pissarro (having lost his friend Cézanne to Provence) turned to a new and much younger generation: the so-called neo-impressionists, chief among them Georges Seurat, to whom Pissarro paid unwavering admiration. At that point, the relationship between Pissarro and Monet couldn't be further apart. In fact, Pissarro referred to his erstwhile colleagues, the impressionists, as "romantics," whereas

Camille Pissarro
La Varenne-Saint-Hilaire,
View from Champigny, c. 1863
[cat. 3]

Fig. 13
Claude Monet
A Field of Poppies, 1873
Oil on canvas, 50 × 65 cm
Musée d'Orsay, Paris, Gift of Etienne
Moreau-Nélaton, 1906, RF 1676

he, together with Seurat and Paul Signac were paving the way toward scientific impressionism, i.e., neo-impressionism.

Thus far, Pissarro had only trusted people who were younger than him: Degas (four years younger), Cézanne (nine years younger), Seurat (twenty-nine years younger). As Pissarro scholar Richard R. Brettell has pointed out, without ever working with a "master" per se, Pissarro benefitted from a long series of "colleagues-teachers-students" collaborations.[3] But his interconnection with Monet does not resemble any of his previous relationships, even though Monet was ten years his junior.

Monet and Pissarro share the fact that they dedicated the last decades of their lives to painting *in series*: indeed, it can be said that the serial practice informed by far the largest part of their production, even though each of them approached the serial concept in a very distinct way. We will examine here how this dual fascination with the idea of painting in series developed in both artists' minds and late careers.

Monet and Pissarro had met in London during the Franco-Prussian War in 1870: Monet was thirty years old; Pissarro was forty. Even though Monet and Pissarro clearly count as the two most important landscape painters among the impressionists [cat. 3 and fig. 13], their approach to the problematic of the representation of nature was notoriously different. Besides, Monet, like Renoir, let himself be lured by the temptations of reaching success through the official Salons, which was anathema for such intransigent minds as Pissarro or Degas.

Their relationship was, therefore, cordial but never very close during the impressionist period. In 1886, towards the end of the impressionist era, things became complicated when Pissarro openly turned his back on classical impressionism (which he dubbed as "romantic" impressionism) while endorsing, with ardent passion, the cause of the "scientific" impressionists, also known as "neo-impressionists" or "pointillists": Seurat and Signac, who were just about his son's age. In fact, his eldest son, Lucien Pissarro (1863–1944), participated in the neo-impressionist exhibitions. At this point, the relationship between Pissarro and Monet became seriously strained.

Though there was a time (1886–90) when it seemed that Pissarro and Monet might not have much to say to each other any longer, a sequence of upsetting events turned around Pissarro's life and his deep faith in *la jeune*

peinture. First, it must be noted that Pissarro's experiment with neo-impressionism, while considered today to be one of the high points of his career, was *then* met with a cold shoulder on the part of critics and collectors; even his dealer had serious doubts about the chances of selling Pissarro's *nouvelle manière*. This new technique – much more complex than a mere accumulation of dot-like brush marks – was very painstaking, and required much longer spans of time to execute a single painting than his prior impressionist technique.

Yet, during the last few years of the 1880s, Pissarro's letters abounded with pejorative statements about impressionism, with which he had completely broken ties. On December 3, 1886, Armand Guillaumin went to visit Pissarro to ask him whether he intended to attend the regular *dîner des impressionnistes*. Pissarro knew nothing of it – he had simply been crossed off the list, possibly by Monet himself.[4] "*Tant pis pour les esprits étroits!*"[5] Pissarro retorted, barely concealing his bitter disappointment in his old comrades. After concluding that impressionism was completely over ("*C'est bien fini, les impressionnistes*"[6]), he ended his letter to Lucien on an angry and threatening note:

Je les attends de pied ferme! Je te prie de croire que notre rôle sera très simple: agir seuls! Nous avons ce qu'il faut pour être forts.[7]

The link between Pissarro and his earlier impressionist colleagues appeared totally broken. Among all of them, it was Monet who, to Pissarro's eye, seemed to incarnate "*l'ancienne exécution si désordonnée,*"[8] which, Pissarro concluded, had become impossible to maintain.[9] In fact, it was almost with these exact terms that a few weeks earlier Pissarro had delivered a terminal and rather cruel verdict on Monet's artistic manner. Supreme irony, Durand-Ruel had asked Pissarro (whose English was fluent) to comment on Monet's paintings to a prospective American buyer called Robertson. Pissarro explained to his son Lucien that he accomplished this request very loyally ("*très loyalement*"[10]), conceding to all the talent of the artist despite the fact that he had gone the wrong way ("*malgré son erreur*"[11]) and appraising the painting of Monet using strongly negative terms. Despite Pissarro's "loyal" comments, Robertson could not get used to Monet's art. Pissarro almost seemed comforted to share Robertson's expression of distaste in front of Monet's works, and he did not hesitate to couch Robertson's "horror" (the term used by Pissarro) in his own terms:

> D'où vient cette horreur? ... Cet homme simple doit être effrayé par le désordre qui ressort de cette fantaisie romanesque qui, malgré le talent de l'artiste, n'est plus en accord avec notre époque.[12]

The relationship with the artist whom he used to refer to as "his old comrade"[13] appeared to have reached an all-time low.

Yet, by the beginning of the 1890s, the situation between the two men turned around again. The successive deaths of Vincent van Gogh (1890), of his brother, art dealer Theo van Gogh (1891), and of Georges Seurat (1891) considerably impacted and upset Pissarro. His faith in the future of the new generation of painters was quite shaken. He also had to face tremendous hardships due to the lack of commercial success of his neo-impressionist production – made all the harder by its time-consuming execution.

On April 1, 1891, Pissarro wrote a very friendly note to Monet, inviting him to the opening of a small show of his works on paper, displayed next to Mary Cassatt's pastels, at Durand-Ruel's gallery. He concluded with a postscript:

> Vous avez appris, probablement, la mort de ce pauvre Seurat, à 31 ans!... n'est-ce point affreux.[14]

The very same day, Pissarro wrote a letter to his son and confidant, Lucien, which he concluded with this summation: "*Je suis allé à l'enterrement de Seurat hier... Je crois que tu as raison, c'est fini le pointillé.*"[15] With Seurat's death, the artistic fate of "*le point*" (the dot) seemed to be over.

The warming up towards Monet did not happen over night, however. At first, Pissarro expressed the greatest skepticism towards Monet's first attempts towards serialism:

> J'ai vu de Bellio hier qui te dit bien des choses. Il m'a annoncé que Monet allait faire une exposition tout seul chez Durand: rien que des Meules; le commis de Boussod et Valadon m'a dit que les amateurs ne demandaient tous que des Meules. Je ne sais comment cela ne gêne pas Monet de s'astreindre à cette répétition... Voilà les effets terribles du succès.[16]

These bitter-sweet remarks turned Monet into a commercial machine – one can almost anticipate here the kind of comments Andy Warhol would share about his own production (except, of course, that from Warhol's perspective, producing art like a machine, for merely lucrative gain, was praiseworthy). These negative feelings about Monet's commercial success were not new. They had, in fact, already been exacerbated during Pissarro's neo-impressionist years when his own commercial success plummeted further than before. His complaint against Monet conjures up Aesop's fable of the sour grapes:

> Je dis ceci: Monet joue son jeu de vendeur, c'est dans son intérêt, moi ce n'est pas dans mon caractère, ni non plus mon intérêt, et surtout pas dans mes idées d'art, je ne suis pas un fantaisiste![17]

In April 1891, Pissarro announced to Lucien, after having expressed wild enthusiasm for "the admirable results" of Miss Cassatt's prints, that he and Cassatt convened to execute some series together: "*c'est convenu avec Mlle. Cassatt de faire ensemble avec elle des séries.*"[18] In the same letter, however, Pissarro lamented his lack of funds – and the fact that the market was all about Monet. All the money went to Monet:

> Pour le moment on ne demande que des Monet. Il paraît qu'il n'en fait pas assez. Le plus terrible, c'est que tous veulent avoir des *Meules au soleil couchant*!!! Toujours la même routine, tout ce qu'il fait part pour l'Amérique à des prix de 4,000 – 5,000 – ou 6,000 francs.[19]

These bemoaning expressions finally came to an end the day Pissarro discovered Monet's "repetitive" series of grainstack paintings in the flesh [figs. 14 and 15]. Pissarro's recurring eye infection continued to bother him, and he attended the opening of Monet's exhibition of fifteen grainstack paintings with an eye patch – thus only discovering Monet's first series with one eye... However, he wrote a remarkably generous and self-searching review of the show. The text deserves citation insofar as it represents a turning point in Pissarro's career and artistic thinking:

> Cela m'a paru très lumineux et très maître, c'est incontestable, mais comme pour notre propre instruction nous devons voir

Fig. 14
Claude Monet
Stacks of Wheat (End of Summer), 1890–91
Oil on canvas, 60 × 100 cm
The Art Institute of Chicago, Chicago, Gift
of Arthur M. Wood, Sr. in memory of Pauline
Palmer Wood, 1985.1103

Fig. 15
Camille Pissarro
Haystacks, Morning, Eragny, 1899
Oil on canvas, 63.5 × 80 cm
The Metropolitan Museum of Art, New York,
Bequest of Douglas Dillon, 2003, 2004.359

Fig. 16
Claude Monet
Boulevard des Capucines, 1873
Oil on canvas, 80.3 × 60.3 cm
Nelson-Atkins Museum of Art, Kansas City,
Missouri, Acquired through the Kenneth
A. and Helen F. Spencer Acquisition Fund

Camille Pissarro
The Place du Havre, Paris, 1893
[cat. 62]

l'au-delà, je me suis demandé ce qui pourrait me sembler manquer; c'est bien difficile à distinguer: ce n'est certes ni dans la justesse, ni dans l'harmonie. Ce serait plutôt dans l'unité de l'exécution que je trouverais à redire, ou plutôt dans une manière plus calme de voir, moins éphémère dans certaines parties: les couleurs sont plutôt jolies que fortes, le dessin est beau, mais flottant dans les fonds surtout.

C'est égal, c'est un bien grand artiste! Inutile de te dire que c'est un grand succès; c'est tellement séduisant que franchement, ce n'est pas étonnant: ce toiles respirent le contentement.[20]

This letter is moving for more reasons than one: not only does it indicate a(n almost) complete aesthetic surrender on Pissarro's part in the face of Monet's supreme artistic achievement and discovery, but, furthermore, it is also an avowal to his son that Monet's practice would from then on serve Pissarro as a gauge, a yardstick for his own artistic practice. Pissarro's program couldn't be clearer: watching in admiration Monet's new pictorial departure led him to question what might be lacking there and how this observation, in turn, could serve his own artistic program.

It didn't take very long for the results of this program to become visible. By December of the same year, Pissarro announced to his son *une belle série de Bazincourt*[21] on its way to completion [PDR 923–930]:

Il a fait un bien beau temps ces jours-ci... froid sec, gelée blanche et soleil radieux... aussi j'ai commencé une série d'études de ma fenêtre, toile de huit, quinze et trente. C'est extraordinaire comme on est sûr de son exécution, et c'est autrement plus facile!... Si je puis les terminer, j'aurai une belle série de Bazincourt. Je craignais que ce ne fût un peu le même motif, mais c'est si varié, les effets, que cela fait des choses toutes différentes; et puis, la coupe y est pour beaucoup.[22]

Summary of 1891

Pissarro began the year by attacking Monet (prior to having seen any of the works of his first series) for being repetitive, *"rien que des Meules."*[23] Grainstacks, nothing but grainstacks, he groaned, from hearsay. By mid-year (May), his discovery of the actual first results of this newly developed serial practice

became something of an epiphany on his own practice. Finally, by the end of the year Pissarro realized that the results of serial practice could be quasi-inexhaustible; far from being repetitive (he was afraid of falling into the same trap as he had anticipated for Monet, early in the year), he found, in fact, that the effects were so varied that each canvas was totally different from the next.

By the end of 1891, Pissarro had discovered for himself the joy of serial practice. Interestingly enough, the letter quoted above is practically never mentioned in the Pissarro literature, as one of the gravest oversights in Pissarro studies consists in having almost completely obliterated the fact that what he referred to as his "Bazincourt series" consists of over three hundred paintings, and, therefore, counts as the largest single "series" executed by any artist of the impressionist generation.[24] One would have to wait for Warhol, again, or Donald Judd and Sol LeWitt to come across such an extensive immersion in serial practices.

If one excepts a group of thirteen paintings executed in 1883 around the Rouen harbor – which count, for Pissarro, as a first, unsystematic attempt at painting in series – the works painted in 1891, depicting the fields that stretched from his studio in Eragny to the next village, Bazincourt, constitute Pissarro's first, fully articulated serial group of paintings.

Soon thereafter, in 1893 Pissarro began doubling up his serial practice by alternating work in rural landscapes (all focusing on the fields and meadows between Eragny and Bazincourt) and cityscapes, starting with Paris [fig. 16 and cat. 62] – the Gare Saint-Lazare series (1893), the Boulevard Montmartre series (1897), the Avenue de l'Opéra series (1898), the Tuileries Gardens series (1899–1900), the Square du Vert-Galant and Pont-Neuf series (1900–2), and the Quai Voltaire series (1903) – moving on to Rouen (1896, 1898) and then Dieppe – the Église Saint-Jacques series (1901) and the Dieppe Harbors series (1902) – and, finally, Le Havre – the Le Havre Harbor series (1903).

Looking solely at Pissarro's production of cityscapes series during the last decade of his life (1893–1903) is daunting in itself. As Brettell summed up the question:

Pissarro painted more cityscapes than any other major impressionist, and, as such, made the most sustained contribution to urban view painting by any great artist since the death of Canaletto in 1768.[25]

Fig. 17
Camille Pissarro
The Roofs of Old Rouen, Gray Weather, 1896
Oil on canvas, 72.3 × 91.4 cm
Toledo Museum of Art, Toledo, Ohio,
Purchased with funds from the Libbey
Endowment, Gift of Edward Drummond Libbey,
1951.361

Fig. 18
Claude Monet
*The Portal of Rouen Cathedral
in Morning Light,* 1894
Oil on canvas, 100.3 × 65.1 cm
The J. Paul Getty Museum,
Los Angeles, 2001.33

Throughout the 1890s, Monet and Pissarro exploited the serial game: they both went at it with a vengeance, with utterly different results. In fact, one can just about imagine what an incredible exhibition would result of bringing together the serial accomplishments of both of these artists within the span of a decade: this would be an extraordinary curatorial feat, with incomparable visual results.

Nonetheless, each artist went about executing his own series in very different ways: together they represent the yin and yang of seriality. Monet confined his practice to landscape motifs with one exception, the Rouen Cathedral. Each of his serial projects was carefully delineated, both temporally and spatially.

Pissarro worked on much longer and less clearly defined spans of time: the so-called "Bazincourt series" has precedents that go back to the first years Pissarro inhabited Eragny, and, therefore, extends over a period of nearly twenty years. Furthermore, unlike Monet, Pissarro shifted radically from the quiet, bucolic silence of the Eragny/Bazincourt meadows to immerse himself in the bustling industrial take-off of late nineteenth-century France – observing the colossal spurts of energy (smoke, steam, smog, clouds) all intermingled with each other, while the toings and froings of the ceaseless streams of traffic (of all kinds) cross each other and form chance-based constellations.

Rouen

The only place where Monet and Pissarro overlapped was Rouen [figs. 17 and 18]. Rouen became, in effect, the battlefield where the two artists tested their serial strategies and fought with all their might. One could say that Pissarro's proto-serial experiments took place in Rouen in 1883 – as stated above – but Monet, who had been brought up in Le Havre, obviously knew Rouen since his childhood. His decision to paint the Rouen Cathedral in 1892 and 1893 was one of the great artistic moves of all times. Twenty of the thirty paintings of the Cathedral were shown at Durand-Ruel's gallery in 1895. The initial interest that Pissarro had expressed for grainstacks, and for poplars, was nothing in comparison to his wild, unbridled enthusiasm for cathedrals. The letter in which Pissarro expresses distress at knowing that his son Lucien will not be able to make it to Monet's *Cathedrals* exhibition speaks volumes (the letter was written on June 1, 1895):

C'est mardi 4 juin que cela ferme, et les vingt *Cathédrales* se disperseront. Et cependant avec un peu d'énergie, tu aurais pu avoir le temps d'être ici à temps. C'est très grand dommage car les *Cathédrales* sont fort discutées, et aussi fort louées par Degas, moi, Renoir et autres. J'aurais tant voulu que tu voies cela *dans son ensemble*, car j'y trouve une unité superbe que j'ai tant cherchée.[26]

The letter goes on: Pissarro vents his anger (seldom does he do this in his correspondence) at his son for being so stupid as to miss the boat (figuratively and literally) and failing to see what the father considered to be one of the greatest exhibitions he had ever visited. In fact, curiously, 1895 offered Pissarro the opportunity to see two of the most important shows of his lifetime: Monet's *Cathedrals* exhibition and the first large-scale retrospective of Cézanne's work that opened at Vollard's gallery.

Note that the tone towards Monet had changed totally: within the span of eight years or so, Monet had moved from the status of an outmoded "*fantaisiste*"[27] artist, bypassed by history, to that of an uncontested master; while Pissarro had looked in Monet's grainstacks for unsolved problems, he found in his cathedrals the solutions he had always sought.

And so, Rouen became the one and only pictorial zone where the two artists confronted each other head on. Within months of the closing of Monet's *Cathedrals* show, Pissarro booked a hotel room, not far from the Cathedral, in Rouen. He arrived there in the last week of February; the weather was damp and cold; the hotel room he found let a bad draft in and was not heated. But he was in heaven and he described the motif of a first painting to Lucien with wild enthusiasm:

J'ai trouvé un motif hors ligne dans une chambre d'hôtel donnant sur le nord; c'est glacial et pas de cheminée. Figure-toi tout le vieux Rouen vu par-dessus les toits, avec la cathédrale, l'église Saint-Ouen, et des fantaisies de toitures, de tourelles, vraiment étonnantes. Vois-tu une toile de trente remplie de toitutres grises, vermoulues, vieilles, c'est extraordinaire![28]

Pissarro is referring here to *The Roofs of Old Rouen, Gray Weather*, the painting in the Toledo Museum – and indeed, one of his chefs-d'oeuvre [fig. 17]. The work almost immediately found a buyer, the rich industrialist François Depeaux, the most important collector in Rouen. But soon, the ever-vexing question of the price difference between Monet and Pissarro came to the fore. Pissarro knew that Depeaux had acquired a

Cathedral from Monet for around 12,000 francs. Pissarro offered him *The Roofs of Old Rouen* painting for 4,000 francs: Depeaux made him an offer for 3,000 francs. Wounded, Pissarro rejected the offer and fell into a self-questioning, semi-depressed mood. After an initial fiery pang of enthusiasm, he felt that he was no good, and that the ever-looming question of his comparison to Monet was one that he would never overcome.

He decided that he was going to keep *The Roofs of Old Rouen, Gray Weather* "for myself" (the Pissarro family) and concluded on this self-deprecatory note:

Je ne l'exposerai pas à cause des cathédrales de Monet: je crains que ce ne soit [pas] assez bon pour soutenir cette comparaison quoique ce soit bien différent: tu sais combien on est médisant.[29]

Hurt to the core, Pissarro resolved never to show this masterful painting, lest it should not "stand the inevitable comparison." The artist held good to his intention: the canvas disappeared from the public eye, staying in the family home until 1903. Upon Pissarro's death, it passed into the hands of his widow, Julie, who gave it, through a deed of gift, to her fourth son, art historian Ludovic-Rodolphe, in the 1920s.

Pissarro not only kept this work out of the public eye, but he almost immediately turned his back on the Cathedral – and metonymically, on Monet's daunting presence in Rouen – and launched feverishly into another series: that of the Rouen bridges [figs. 19–21 and cat. 78]. The Cathedral was all but dead for Pissarro.

Unlike science fiction, art history fiction hardly exists. But, let us imagine for a few seconds that Depeaux had accepted to pay the price Pissarro asked for *The Roofs of Old Rouen, Gray Weather*. Pissarro's mood and self-confidence would have been considerably boosted, and, more than likely, a whole series of Rouen and its old roofs, with the Cathedral in the background, would have come out of this. An extraordinary complement to Monet's *Cathedral* series would have come to fruition, one in which, as in the Toledo Museum painting, the Cathedral would not be floating in an ethereal polychromatic atmospheric cloud [Monet's *Cathedrals*], but would be anchored in a sea of wobbling roofs, covered by moss, weathered by time. But this did not happen.

Pissarro's review of the *Cathedral* exhibition is among the salient pieces of art literature written by one of the impressionists. As soon as the show opened, Pissarro wrote

Fig. 19
Camille Pissarro
The Great Bridge, Rouen, 1896
Oil on canvas, 74 × 92 cm
Carnegie Museum of Art, Pittsburgh, Purchase, 00.9

Fig. 21
Camille Pissarro
Pont Boieldieu in Rouen, Rainy Weather, 1896
Oil on canvas, 73.6 × 91.4 cm
Art Gallery of Ontario, Toronto, Gift of Reuben Wells Leonard Estate, 1937

Fig. 20
Camille Pissarro
Pont Boieldieu, Rouen, Sunset, Misty Weather, 1896
Oil on canvas, 54 × 65 cm
Musée des Beaux-Arts, Rouen, on long-term loan from
the Musée d'Orsay, Paris, 1983, RF 1983–7

Camille Pissarro
*The Pont Boieldieu and the Pont Corneille,
Rouen, Effect of Rain*, 1896
[cat. 78]

to his son. He went to see the exhibition probably more often than he ever saw any other show, and kept lamenting the fact that Lucien was not making plans to return from London in order to visit the exhibit in Paris. Almost two weeks after the show opened, Pissarro wrote:

> Je regretterais que tu ne sois ici avant la fermeture de l'exposition de Monet; ses *Cathédrales* vont être dispersées d'un côté et d'autre, et c'est surtout dans son ensemble qu'il faut que ce soit vu. C'est très combattu par les jeunes et même par des admirateurs de Monet. Je suis très emballé par cette maîtrise extraordinaire. Cézanne, que j'ai rencontré hier chez Durand, est bien de mon avis que c'est l'œuvre d'un volontaire, bien pondéré, poursuivant l'insaisissable nuance des effets que ne vois réalisée par aucun artiste. Quelques artistes nient la nécessité de cette recherche; personnellement, je trouve toutes recherches légitimes, quand c'est senti à ce point.[30]

The following year, in 1896, collector Depeaux's refusal to pay more for Pissarro's own Cathedral floating on a tumultuous volume of ruddy roofs put an end to Pissarro's interest in further exploring the same theme. The wound to his self-esteem was too harsh and bitter. The same man who would pay 12,000 francs for one of Monet's *Cathedrals* refused to pay more than a quarter of that sum for Pissarro's own. For a bit more, for a third of that price (4,000 francs), the collector could have acquired this work. But no. The two men, the artist and the collector, refused to budge.

His pride considerably hurt, Pissarro decided to look at the other side of the Rouen medal. With the exception of three works depicting the Rue de l'Épicerie leading up to the Cathedral, Pissarro focused his artistic attention on the *other* Rouen: the Cathedral was all about verticality, and its thrusting vertical axes were pointing to the ether, to some kind of eternity (difficult to define from the perspective of an atheist, as Monet was).

Pissarro instead focused on the city's vast expanses of horizontality, the powerful industrial vectors that gave the new Rouen its physiognomy as one of the central hubs of a fast growing web of economic exchange and production in late nineteenth-century Europe. And so, the Rouen that consumed Pissarro's artistic passion was the anti-Monetian Rouen: no trace of the medieval past in the new bridges that established a criss-crossing network over the river Seine – itself the umbilical cord between the capital of France and one of the largest industrial and commercial harbors of Europe, Le Havre.

Le Havre

Le Havre: another interesting meeting point in the destinies of these artists, Monet and Pissarro. The beginning for one; the end for the other.

Monet was five years old when his parents moved from Paris to Le Havre: he not only grew up there, but went to his first art school there too. Coincidentally, Le Havre was also the city where Pissarro first set foot on French soil after having crossed the Atlantic Ocean, aged twelve, from his native Saint Thomas.

Le Havre was also the city where Pissarro accomplished his last series, outside Paris, with some outstanding results. One of them – one of the last paintings listed and illustrated in the artist's catalogue raisonné [PDR 1520] – appears to tie in with the various circles that formed the complicated though fascinating artistic lives of Monet and Pissarro.

At the age of seventy-three, Pissarro found himself once again in Le Havre, where he continued searching for new motifs, new sources of inspiration for his series. He knew, of course, that Le Havre was Monet's city, the city where Monet had come of age as an artist. And he remembered that he had been twelve years old when he first stepped off one of those transatlantic steamers which he saw, day in, day out, and that he had been twenty-five years old when for the last time he stepped down from one of these steamers in 1855, having decided to settle permanently in France in order to become an artist.

Gazing at this transatlantic traffic, Pissarro could not but reminisce on the early trajectories that bound both artists together: even though Monet was only fifteen years old when Pissarro set foot for the second time in Le Havre, ironically the city was a stepping stone for both men. And for Pissarro, it was also a final destination in his own serial race.

> Je vois passer devant ma fenêtre toute la journée les grands steamers transatlantiques et autres du matin au soir, avec les docks, le traffic: c'est grandiose; je crois que je tiens une série nouvelle qui sera intéressante.[31]

The letter was sent the day after the artist's seventy-third birthday – his last.

1. "My dear Pissarro, I am very sorry to learn that you are sick, and I hope that, with good care, you will soon be restored to good health. As for your concerns about your old debt, you need no longer worry about it in the least, you know very well that Durand-Ruel paid me back in full a long time ago. So take care of yourself without fretting over the matter and let me have your news. [...] Yours, with all my heart, and my best regards to all your family. Your devoted, Claude Monet." Letter from Claude Monet to Camille Pissarro, November 9, 1903, The Getty Center for the History of Art and the Humanities, Archives of the History of Art; published in *Correspondance de Camille Pissarro*, ed. Janine Bailly-Herzberg, 5 vols. [vol. 1: 1865–85; vol. 2: 1886–90; vol. 3: 1891–94; vol. 4: 1895–98; and vol. 5: 1899–1903] (Saint-Ouen-l'Aumône: Valhermeil, 1986–91), vol. 5, pp. 384–85 (henceforward referred to as *Correspondance*).

2. "your old debt."

3. Richard R. Brettell, "Camille Pissarro and Fritz Melbye: Two Painters 'sans maître'," in *Pissarro: Critical Catalogue of Paintings*, 3 vols. (Milan: Skira; Paris: Wildenstein Institute, 2005), vol. 1, p. 5.

4. *Correspondance*, vol. 2, p. 80, December 3, 1886.

5. Ibid: "So much the worse for the narrow-minded!" English translation from Camille Pissarro, *Letters to his Son Lucien*, ed. John Rewald, trans. Lionel Abel (New York: Pantheon, 2nd ed., 1943), p. 83 (henceforward referred to as *Letters to his Son*).

6. Ibid: "The impressionists are done for."

7. Ibid: "I await them without wavering! Please understand that our role is very simple: we must stand alone! We have the stuff to be strong."

8. *Correspondance*, vol. 2, p. 120, January 23, 1887: "the old disorderly method of execution." *Letters to his Son*, p. 97.

9. Ibid.

10. Ibid: "loyally and without hesitation."

11. Ibid: "despite his mistakes."

12. Ibid, p. 101, January 9, 1887: "And who painted this horror ?"... But this simple man must be offended by the disorder which results from a type of romantic fantasy which despite the talent of the artist, is not in accord with the spirit of our time." *Letters to his Son*, p. 91.

13. Ibid, p. 40.

14. Ibid, vol. 3, p. 53: "You have probably heard of the death of poor Seurat, at the age of 31! [...] isn't it dreadful."

15. Ibid, p. 54, April 1, 1891: "Yesterday I went to Seurat's funeral ... I believe you are right, pointillism is finished." *Letters to his Son*, p. 158.

16. Ibid, p. 61, April 9, 1891: "I saw de Bellio yesterday; he sends you his best. He mentioned that Monet was going to have a one-man show at Durand-Ruel's, and exhibit *nothing but Sheaves*. The clerk at Boussod et Valadon told me that the collectors want only *Sheaves*. I don't understand how Monet can submit to this demand that he repeat himself – such is the terrible consequence of success!" *Letters to his Son*, p. 161.

17. Ibid, vol. 2, p. 101, January 9, 1887: "I say this: Monet plays his salesman's game, and it serves him; but it is not in my character to do likewise, nor is it to my interest, and it would be in contradiction above all to my conception of art. I am not a romantic!" *Letters to his Son*, p. 92.

18. Ibid, vol. 3, p. 55, April 3, 1891: "incidentally I have agreed to do a series with Miss Cassatt." *Letters to his Son*, p. 158.

19. Ibid: "But for the moment people want nothing but Monets, apparently he can't paint enough pictures to meet the demand. Worst of all they all want *Sheaves in the Setting Sun*! Always the same story, everything he does goes to America at prices of four, five and six thousand francs." *Letters to his Son*, p. 159.

20. Ibid, p. 72, May 5, 1891: "They seemed to me to be very luminous and very masterful, that was very evident, but as for our own development we ought to see deeper, I asked myself: what do they lack? Something very difficult to delimit clearly. Certainly in rightness and harmony they leave nothing to be desired; it would rather be in the unity of execution that I would find something to be improved, or rather I should prefer a calmer, less fleeting mode of vision in certain parts. The colors are pretty rather than strong, the drawing is good but wavering – particularly in the backgrounds – just the same, this is the work of a very great artist. Need I add that the show is a great success? This is not surprising, considering how attractive the works are. These canvases breathe contentment." *Letters to his Son*, p. 166.

21. "a beautiful series of Bazincourt paintings."

22. Ibid, p. 175, December 26, 1891: "We are having wonderful weather, these days ... dry cold, hoar-frost and radiant sunlight. I have begun a series of studies from my window, canvases of about 18 × 15, 25 × 21 and 36 × 28 inches. It is extraordinary how certain I am of my execution, which is now much easier. If I finish them I will have a beautiful series of Bazincourt paintings. I was afraid that repetition of the same motif would be tiring, but the effects are so varied that everything is completely transformed, and then the compositions and angles are so different." *Letters to his Son*, p. 192.

23. "nothing but Sheaves."

24. Richard R. Brettell and I are planning an exhibition that will, for the first time, look into the richness and complexity of Pissarro's abiding dedication to this single series project.

25. Richard R. Brettell, "Camille Pissarro and Urban View Painting: An Introduction," in Richard R. Brettell and Joachim Pissarro, *The Impressionist and the City: Pissarro's Series Paintings* [exh. cat. Dallas Museum of Art, November 15, 1992–January 31, 1993; Philadelphia Museum of Art, March 7–June 6, 1993; Royal Academy of Art, London, July 2–October 10, 1993] (New Haven: Yale University Press, 1992), p. XV.

26. *Correspondance*, vol. 4, p. 78, June 1, 1895: "I arrived in Paris today expecting to see you, but I see from your letter that you will leave too late to see the Monets. This is a great pity, for the *Cathedrals* are being much talked of, and highly praised, too, by Degas, Renoir, myself and others. I would have so liked you to see the whole series in a group, for I find in it the superb unity which I have been seeking for a long time." *Letters to his Son*, p. 270.

27. "romantic."

28. *Correspondance*, vol. 4, p. 168, February 26, 1896: "I think I shall stay here until the end of March, for I found a really uncommon motif in a room of the hotel facing north, ice-cold and without a fireplace. Just conceive for yourself: the whole of old Rouen seen from above the rooftops, with the Cathedral, St Ouen's church, and the fantastic roofs, really amazing turrets. Can you picture a canvas about 36 × 28 inches in size, filled with old, gray, worm-eaten roofs? It is extraordinary!" *Letters to his Son*, p. 283.

29. Ibid, p. 173, March 17, 1896: "I don't want to show it on account of Monet's *Cathedrals*, I'm afraid it isn't good enough to stand the inevitable comparison, although it is quite different. You know how much back biting is going on." *Letters to his Son*, p. 284.

30. Ibid, p. 75, May 26, 1895: "If only you could get here before Monet's show closes; his *Cathedrals* will be scattered everywhere, and these particularly ought to be seen in a group. They have been attacked by the young painters and even by Monet's admirers. I am carried away by their extraordinary deftness. Cézanne, whom I met yesterday at Durand-Ruel's, is in complete agreement with my view that this is the work of a well balanced but impulsive artist who pursues the intangible nuances of effects that are realized by no other painter. Certain painters deny the necessity of this research, personally I find any research legitimate that is felt to such a point." *Letters to his Son*, p. 269.

31. *Correspondance*, vol. 5, pp. 357–58, July 11, 1903: "I see the big transatlantic steamers and other boats passing beneath my window all day long, from morning to night, with the docks, the traffic: it's splendid; I think I have a new series in mind which should be interesting."

Richard R. Brettell

Pissarro and Anarchism: Can Art be Anarchist?

"Je crois fermement que nos idées imprégnées
de philosophie anarchique se déteignent sur nos œuvres
et dès lors (elles sont) antipathiques aux idées courantes."

Camille Pissarro, letter to his son Lucien,
April 13, 1891[1]

Camille Pissarro
The Haymaker, 1884
[cat. 44 detail]

Fig. 22
Camille Pissarro
Hay Harvest at Eragny, 1893
Watercolor and gouache on silk, 13 × 25.6 cm
Archives L&S Pissarro Collection, Paris

Richard R. Brettell

Pissarro and Anarchism: Can Art be Anarchist?

In the autumn of 1893, Pissarro sent a beautiful – and hitherto unpublished – gouache-on-silk fan-shaped painting [fig. 22] to the daughter of his faithful dealer, Paul Durand-Ruel, on the occasion of her marriage. His own career had emerged from a period of profound crisis as a direct result of a retrospective exhibition – his first in almost a decade – held at the Durand-Ruel Gallery in Paris in January and February of 1892. The artist was then already sixty-two years old, and, in the next years, his career would take off with the support and guidance of Durand-Ruel and with what was to become Pissarro's new commitment to urban series paintings. This wedding present was for a young woman of means, whose father had been the first major dealer to represent the impressionists and to sell their work to collectors both inside and outside of France. The Durand-Ruel family was, by 1893, wealthy and successful, and lived in grand style as members of a true cosmopolitan bourgeoisie. The recipient of this gouache was, thus, a privileged young woman to whom the painter (who was neither French nor Catholic [or even Christian], and who had only recently been able to purchase the small farm on which he lived with a loan from Monet) was a decidedly marginal figure in French society.

Pissarro could have selected among hundreds of works on silk and paper from throughout his long career for the wedding present. Instead, he created something new, based in part on two paintings from 1889, *Peasants Chatting in the Farmyard, Eragny* [PDR 868] (then still owned by the artist) and *The Gleaners* [PDR 869], which had been purchased from the painter by Durand-Ruel's rival, Boussod et Valadon, in the year it was painted and soon sold, thus not available to Pissarro in 1893.[2] Clearly, he composed the figures in this rural grain harvest from those he had already drawn and created from varied sources – a "new" figural composition based not on something he witnessed in this way, but something ideal. What is interesting is the imagery – a grain harvest in which seven figures, five women and two men, work collectively and without supervision. They are dressed simply as rural workers would be, and they work at what looks today like sunset. It is possible, indeed likely, that the silk on which Pissarro painted the scene has darkened from a light tan to a warm brown, and, since the gouache is applied in such a way that a good deal of the silk support shows through, the entire fan seems suffused with an orange light. Whatever the time of day, they work in what is a beautiful and immense landscape of rolling hills,

fields, and distant forests with no demarcations of property and no buildings of any kind. They are thus embodiments of a kind of "ideal" rural work – which is collective, property-less, and consensual – with no owner, no boss, and, hence, no hierarchy. There is a division of the sexes, with men doing the more difficult labor of scything the grain, while women gather the shafts into sheaves. Some bend to do the work, while the two primary figures stand proudly erect as they stretch their backs and chat before resuming their work.

Could there be a greater contrast between the kind of life of Marie Aube, the recipient of this fan, and the world of collective, classless labor evoked so beautifully on it? She – with her Parisian apartment and access to a bourgeois country house, her servants and fashionable attire, her leisurely life – would have looked at this golden evocation of the joys of collective rural work as another world, utterly apart from hers. We have no idea where or indeed whether it hung in her apartment, but, in any imaginable case, it would have contrasted *not* as art but as political embodiment with her correct bourgeois life. Pissarro was an acknowledged anarchist by the time he made that gift to the daughter of his dealer, and he would never have thought that he made it with any explicit criticism – he was quieter and more persistent in his methods than that. Yet, when he gave it to her, he was working actively for the cause of anarchism, was known by the French police as a practicing anarchist, and had completed the single most powerful embodiment of anti-bourgeois anarchist philosophy ever created by an artist – the handmade book *Turpitudes Sociales* (Social Disgraces), which I will discuss later. Given all of this, we must consider his gift of this fan as a statement of his own philosophy – not as a criticism of her life, but as an embodied ideal of what he imagined all life would be after what all practicing anarchists in Europe felt would be an inevitable social revolution.

Pissarro had been known for decades as an anarchist artist and linked with the artistic practice of more "overtly" anarchist artists like his friends Paul Signac and Maximilian Luce.[3] Yet, conventional art historians, uninterested in politics and comfortable in the utterly bourgeois art world of the twentieth and twenty-first centuries, have often stressed that Pissarro's anarchism was "left at the door" of his studio, in which he serenely practiced a healing modernism without the bite seen in the work of other committed artists like Luce. That this view is wrong takes only one sentence from Pissarro – the one quoted at the opening of this essay. Admittedly, it was written at the very lowest moment of his career, before the Durand-Ruel exhibition that brought it to life in a capitalist world, but its clarity and simplicity had little to do with his current economic woes. Rather, it stemmed from long-fought and hard-won moral beliefs in the primacy of the free individual as the sole building block of a successful society – an individual unfettered by constraints from a society that sanctified private property and wealth above all else, even above the family. Whatever their difference in political philosophy, Pissarro admired his dealer's commitment to family and to an honest family business. He was also profoundly grateful to him for aiding him materially, so that his own family could profit as a group. But that did not mean that he offered up a view of the beauties of bourgeois society for the Durand-Ruel family's delectation. Instead, he gave them embodied ideals of a world utterly different from theirs and devoted to principles of physical work and collective, mutually satisfying effort.

What are the origins of Pissarro's anarchism? Pissarro writers have stressed his rejection of the utterly bourgeois values of his own family, which, like many modern Jewish families, was focused around business and measured success in money and property. Pissarro's rejection of those values was complete, and it is clear even from his rare early letters that he valued a property-less life with few possessions and a commitment to work. For him, the making of art was at odds with conventional bourgeois society in spite of the fact that its markets were controlled by bourgeois forces. It was precisely the freedom of the artist from conventional life and all the associations of what was then called "bohemia" that attracted Pissarro to a non-mercantile life-style and mode of production. Yet, even by the 1860s, we know that Pissarro began to move in anarchist and proto-anarchist circles and that he, together with his friend Ludovic Piette, began systematically to read political and social theory at a time when it was severely constrained by systematic state censorship. After the death of his father in 1865 and his assumption of an unsanctioned relationship with his mother's servant, his future wife, Julie Vellay, he associated with Gustav Courbet, an overtly political artist, and rejected his own religious traditions – indeed all organized religion. We do not know whether Pissarro was involved even peripherally in the worker's movements that crystallized in the First International in 1868. He left Paris for what was to be the "try-out" of the great revolution in the

Commune of 1871, thereby missing the collapse of communal government both from its own failures and from its systematic repression by nationalist forces led by president Adolphe Thiers. Pissarro tended to read rather than riot and to make art which embodied aspects of the world of contemporary France that conformed to his own ideal of a property-less state enshrining individual freedom and small-scale collective decision making without the hierarchic bureaucracy of a central government. Indeed, his only independent representation of an urban demonstration, a slight but accomplished drawing in the collection of the Dallas Museum of Art [fig. 24], remains an anomaly in his early career.

What seems to have been Camille Pissarro's first clearly "political" painting, the *Donkey Ride at La Roche-Guyon* [fig. 23], was signed but not dated by the artist, forcing us to assign the picture a date on the basis of style alone.[4] It is of modest dimensions (not a Salon painting) and attractive, at least at first glance. Yet, the more we look at it, the clearer it becomes that its social message – an excoriating contrast between social classes, between the "haves" and "have-nots" sharing an attractive agricultural landscape near the historic French town of La Roche-Guyon – is a political one. Apparently, the pair of young children on the left is parentless and probably vagabond, their ragged, hand-me-down clothing serving as a talisman of their social degradation. What one takes to be the little girl wears a coat that is painted to match with the new one on the little rich boy on the donkey, thereby emphasizing its inappropriateness for her. These children are diametrically opposed to the two well-dressed bourgeois children sitting on the donkeys' backs – probably rented for an hour or so on a nice summer day. Far from alone, they are in the company of a well-dressed woman who is probably their mother rather than a nanny, and the fact that each child sits astride a donkey is a clear indication of their status as members of the leisure class or bourgeoisie. It is not an accident that Pissarro places them on rented donkeys rather than small horses, and the associations of the donkeys with a kind of braying stupidity was surely in his mind in spite of the fact that the scene is represented in a way that is completely plausible.

Clearly the painting dates from the 1860s, the first full decade in Pissarro's French life, and we know that he spent time in La Roche-Guyon in 1864 and may have gone with his friend, the natty Antoine Guillemet, in September of 1865. It is

Fig. 23
Camille Pissarro
Donkey Ride at La Roche-Guyon, c. 1865
Oil on canvas, 35 × 51.7 cm
Private collection

perhaps for that reason, together with the appearance later in the year of Pierre-Joseph Proudhon's *Du Principe de l'art et de sa destination sociale* (On the Principles of Art and its Social Function), that Joachim Pissarro and other scholars (myself included) date the picture to those years. We suspect that Pissarro moved in politically radical circles in the late 1860s, but we have very few details about them or about his friendship with known political figures such as Elie and Elisée Reclus or Aristide Rey, all three of whom he knew later. The rigor of French national censorship during the Second Empire was such that, in spite of a comparative rise in Communist, Anarcho-Communist, and Socialist political practice in France, most of this was accomplished in a clandestine manner to avoid police suspicion, and many radical publications of this and the later period were produced in Switzerland and England, where press freedom was greater than in France.

Given the absence of documentary details about the formation of Pissarro's early political ideas, one must turn to this painting and to the important if uninspiring text by Proudhon, which many think induced Pissarro to make this modest political statement and, perhaps, his only early drawing representing a political rally in France, *Urban Uprising in Paris* (not Pissarro's title), in the Reves Collection at the Dallas Museum of Art, which is usually dated to 1870 [fig. 24], before the artist fled France for safety in England. All we can say from this small painting is that Pissarro had decided that art was an arena in which advanced ideas about politics could be played out. In this he followed the general dictum of Proudhon, who exhorted artists, using the commanding example of Courbet, to abandon the representation of ideal worlds – whether mythological, religious, or historical – to confront directly the contemporary world with all its contradictions and problems. He also sought an art that embodied enduring values of individual liberty and equality, and there is ample evidence that Pissarro shared these views, although he does not write positively about the works of Proudhon until much later in his life.

It is not really until his sons began to leave home and gain independence that Pissarro started to write the letters which have become a bedrock of impressionist studies. In some ways, Pissarro's missives have played a larger role in the study of impressionism than have his works of art, because of their reliability and clarity and because they report directly about such seminal artists as Monet, Renoir, Degas, Cézanne,

Fig. 24
Camille Pissarro
Urban Uprising in Paris, 1870
Charcoal, wash and gouache
on wove paper, 343 × 381 mm
The Dallas Museum of Art, The Wendy
and Emery Reves Collection, 1985.R.49

Fig. 25
Camille Pissarro
Still Life, 1867
Oil on canvas, 81 × 99.6 cm
Toledo Museum of Art, Toledo, Ohio, 1949.6

Gauguin, Seurat, and others. Their selflessness and wide-ranging inquiries into the complex world of galleries, critics, museums, artists, journalism, politics, and money make them a veritable font of primary material for the critic and historian of modern art. What they do *not* do, however, is to attempt any readings of particular works of Pissarro's art. In this, they are different from the letters of Van Gogh or Gauguin, which have been mined for generations as we attempt to interpret specific works of art. Pissarro literally *never* explicates a work in terms of ideas, and, for that reason, this essay will be structured as a series of mini-interpretations of a small group of his works in terms of the anarchist political philosophy to which he referred in the letter quoted at the opening of this essay.

Let us begin with a large and important still life, Pisarro's first major work in this genre, aggressively signed and dated 1867 in the upper right corner and now in the Toledo Museum of Art [fig. 25]. If there is a more elemental still life in French art than this one, it is difficult to identify. Composed in stark bands strictly parallel to the picture plane, the painting presents us with a still life of food and wine that is, at its root, elemental and almost crude. The wine is a deep, dark purplish red served in a simple glass pitcher rather than an elegant crystal decanter. The glass too is thick and common, half-filled with wine. The meal-for-one evoked in the painting (there is only one glass) consists of a trio of small yellow apples which seem to have come from a nearby tree rather than a shop, half a loaf of bread (not the *baguette* familiar from corner bakeries but a thicker, larger loaf that has been cut with a knife in precisely the quantity needed), and a small piece of meat (a ham or even a knuckle of meat with a fatty rind) that sits inelegantly on a thick, painted earthenware plate that is clearly hand-made and hand-painted. There are no chairs, no paintings, no luxury goods, nothing that is not essential and ordinary, and what we take from this painting – which is, in itself, "worked" in thick paint with a palette knife – is that it is a worker's meal in a worker's house, the only "ornament" of which is the glassware, two pewter kitchen spoons, and an irregular painted ceramic plate. Nothing that is not essential is included, and one suspects that the wine comes not from a vintner's bottle but from a cask acquired for little money locally or traded with a friend. Cézanne had made similar still lifes as early as 1865, but none of them have the determined elemental strength of this, one of Pissarro's greatest and most powerful paintings. Surely, it is a visual hymn to a world

Fig. 26
Camille Pissarro
Houses at Bougival (Autumn), 1870
Oil on canvas, 88.9 × 116.2 cm
The J. Paul Getty Museum, Los Angeles, 82.PA.73

without commodities and luxury goods, a world in which what is made by hand – including art – is better than what is elegant, refined, anonymous, and expensive. When we look at Pissarro's contemporary paintings of the working landscape in the cluster of houses knwon as the Hermitage, we can easily imagine that all we would need to do is enter a humble rural abode in one of them to find such a meal awaiting us.

Let us turn next to a major landscape painting, large by Pissarro standards and undoubtedly painted for the Salon of 1870, the year in which it was signed and dated [fig. 26]. Today in the Getty Museum in Los Angeles, it has recently – and mistakenly – been retitled as *Houses at Bougival (Autumn)*, although it was clearly painted in the nearby village of Louveciennes less than a five-minute walk from Pissarro's rented house on the Route de Versailles.[5] Pissarro sent two landscapes to the Salon that year, giving them the elemental titles *Autumn* and *Landscape*. These pictures were discussed in some detail (though not enough to identify them conclusively) by Théodore Duret (in *L'Électeur Libre*) and Zacharie Astruc (in *L'Écho des Beaux-Arts*) and conjured up by Jean Ravenel (in *Revue Internationale de l'Art et de la Curiosité*) as evocations of a "gentle, harmonious whole." Duret, while severe on Pissarro's lack of idealization and his acceptance of ordinary places as they were, actually understood Pissarro's aims precisely when he described his work as paintings of "insignificant settings where nature itself is so un-picturesque that the artist has painted a landscape without making a picture."[6]

This is precisely what Pissarro intended and succeeded in doing with remarkable skill. One can see clearly that he has abandoned the palette knife and its troweled finish for a much more refined and complex surface of small touches of paint that evoke foliage, figures, architecture, and light in such a way that the viewer's eye itself flickers across the plane. The very quotidian nature of the subject – at once suburban and rural – is part of Pissarro's pictorial ideology of modest, communal life without luxury and with the participation of all in what one might call the work of living. In this case, his central figures are a mother and her young son who is simply dressed, but clearly on his way to school with his satchel (could it be Mme. Pissarro with her pail of water or milk and the couple's son, Lucien, who had just turned seven in the early months of 1870, when the picture was finished for submission to the Salon held in May?). The idea of universal

education, so important to anarchist theory and to the Pissarro family, is so subtly introduced into the landscape that one could easily overlook it, but it is no less important for this. For anarchists, a commitment to continued intellectual and moral improvement was as important as working in the fields and the factories of a modern collective world, and Pissarro expressed this in his first truly impressionist Salon landscape. And it is no accident that the artist screened the tower of the modest Louveciennes Catholic church so that it plays an almost residual role in his landscape of work and education.

Although anarchist theory – like that of communism and socialism at the same time – grappled with industrial technology and its role in a property-less modern world, Pissarro himself had not lived in a landscape touched by these "improvements" until an *usine à gaz* was inaugurated in central Pontoise in 1867. Pissarro included the tall smokestack of the gasworks in two paintings and a drawing of 1867–68, but it was not until the painter's return to the landscape of Pontoise in 1872 that he was forced to confront large-scale industrial incursions into "his" landscape. In 1872, M. Châlons, a businessman and investor, purchased a large-flat agricultural field directly across the Oise River from Pissarro's rented home in the hamlet of the Hermitage.[7] Over the next two years, he constructed a large multi-shed factory with four large smokestacks that refined sugar from beets. The location of the factory, adjacent to large fields suitable for beet growing and next to the canalized Oise River and the relatively newly constructed railroad, was clearly strategic, and, for a committed anarchist, it forced Pissarro to measure his own developing ideas about private property and collective work against the realities of industrial capitalism. He did so in the best way a painter could – by depicting the factory in various ways from various angles, in order to integrate it into the landscape.

Of the four paintings from 1873, the year of the factory's opening, the one most commonly reproduced and discussed in print is *The River Oise near Pontoise* [fig. 27] at the Sterling and Francine Clark Art Institute in Williamstown, Massachusetts. This picture is, as I have shown elsewhere, a highly idealized representation of a landscape in which the actual factory buildings and their smokestacks dominated the landscape to a considerably great extent – almost to the point of denying the agricultural character of the area. Clearly, for Pissarro, industry was as essential a part of the new world as it was for the theorists Peter Kropotkin and Elisée Reclus.

However, he struggled to create a pictorial world in which the factory was "balanced" within what Ravenel had earlier called a "gentle, harmonious whole." Here too, Pissarro was steeped in what he himself called the philosophy of anarchism, even at this early stage, and, like the most persuasive theorists of his time, had to consider industry as well as agriculture in the totality of modern working life. What Kropotkin was to call the agro-industrial ideal in which workers spent several months per season working in the fields, while they devoted the other months to other kinds of work in factories, ports, studios, workshops, etc., Pissarro evoked in his Clark canvas, which, in this sense, is an anarchist landscape.

We turn next to his first truly important pictorial evocation of a collective grain harvest, *The Harvest* [fig. 28], a large oil and tempera painting on silk dating from 1882 now in the collection of the National Museum of Western Art in Tokyo, and first shown in the Impressionist Exhibition of 1882.[8] Here, Pissarro created a landscape that stretches as far as the eye can see both in depth and width. It is a scene of fecundity and simplicity that is based loosely on the actual landscape of Pontoise viewed from the vast fields of Saint-Ouen-l'Aumône across the Oise from it. In the distance, we see the rolling hills of the Vexin crowned by a large house that resembles the château of Pontoise itself. Huddled at its base is a simple village of whitewashed houses with red roofs that has more to do with the illustrations in children's books than it does with the industrial town of Pontoise as it was in Pissarro's life. Again, we see a "reality" that is adapted to its pictorial context to form an ideal. Clearly, Pissarro's pictorial *and* social theories had evolved since 1870, when he painted the Getty landscape as a hymn to quotidian village life as it actually was. In this almost equally large and ambitious figure painting, Pissarro created a collective landscape with no clear demarcations of property (there are no fences or other boundaries in its vast agricultural plane), peopled by an equal number of men and women who work together without any apparent supervision. He does not paint the exhausted, wage-earning workers with their boss as Léon Lhermitte did in the same year for his Salon painting, *Paying the Harvesters*, now at the Musée d'Orsay in Paris. Whereas Lhermitte painted a "real" situation in which rural workers, spent at the end of their day of toil, sit in the courtyard of a large farm while the farmer pays them before they go home, there is no money, no landowner, no hierarchy in Pissarro's supremely anarchist – if ideal – world

Fig. 27
Camille Pissarro
The River Oise near Pontoise, 1873
Oil on canvas, 45.3 × 55 cm
The Sterling and Francine Clark Art Institute,
Williamstown, 1955.554

Fig. 28
Camille Pissarro, *The Harvest*, 1882. Oil and tempera on silk, 70.3 × 126 cm
The National Museum of Western Art, Tokyo, P.1984–0003

of equality and shared plenty. This is a world familiar to any reader of Peter Kropotkin, who had extolled the kitchen gardeners and rural workers in the Île de France, suggesting that they produced food for an entire metropolitan area without backbreaking work through small-scale cultivation and shared activity. Pissarro evoked this world in paint as well as Kropotkin did in words.

In the same show of 1882, Pissarro displayed a large group of figure paintings that, collectively, portrayed the very rural workers so carefully studied by Kropotkin in his various writings of the 1870s and 1880s. They represent peasants weeding, picking apples, resting, chatting, tending animals, and going about other mundane tasks. Most of these villagers are female, young and attractive, wearing simple, often hand-spun clothing with both pride and an innate sense of beauty. These figures contributed to create a collective portrait of modern French society at the 1882 exhibition where Renoir focused on the urban working class and the bourgeoisie, and Caillebotte stuck to his own class, the urban haute

bourgeoisie. Yet one picture entitled *Washerwoman, Study* [fig. 29], now at the Metropolitan Museum in New York, occupied a special place in the show because it was a portrait of a working class woman, seated comfortably as she posed decorously for Pissarro. She has long been identified as Marie Larchevêque, and the recent archival research of Claire Durand-Ruel and her colleagues at the Wildenstein Institute has established that a woman with that name was, in fact, a neighbor of the Pissarros in the late 1870s and early 1880s. Although she had no money to commission the portrait and never owned it, she is represented as seriously and respectfully as if she was a member of the moneyed haute bourgeoisie with the means to commission a finished, full-scale oil portrait. Her three-quarter seated pose is like that of literally thousands of her social "betters," who sat for expensive painters during her lifetime. And in making such a portrait, Pissarro used art as a gracious embodiment of the ordinary, demonstrating through art that all people are equally worthy of individual representation. In this, his painting is different from those of hundreds of his contemporaries who portrayed "peasants" not as individuals, but as members of a group without identity and even without name.

It is clear from this simple discussion of various specific works by Pissarro that they are indeed permeated with his reading of anarchist philosophy and with his lifelong search for a morally driven pictorial world, whether rooted in his own direct experience of place or evoking an idealized, better world. He did *not* paint evil, greed, gluttony, selfishness, or superstition – perhaps largely because these evils were, in fact, difficult to embody in pictorial form, since his idea of art was, as our critic from 1870 already said, a "gentle, harmonious whole." Yet, at one point in his career he broke these representational rules and created – with the help of his son Lucien – a unique book with illustrations by himself, texts excerpted from anarchist literature, and binding by Lucien [fig. 30]. As indicated by its title, *Turpitudes Sociales* (Social Disgraces), it represents the evils of capitalist society in a way that is so powerful and intentionally crude that it is extraordinary in the oeuvre of an artist who specialized in gentle harmony. Its intended audience – the two daughters of Pissarro's half-sister – were already in their thirties when the book was made, and Pissarro was afraid that their philosophical/moral development in England was such that they had grown too used to the capitalist world and inured both to its evils and to the extent of its corruption of society when conceived as a whole.

Interestingly, Pissarro used his thorough knowledge of the illustrated press and its stylistic conventions to create a style of black-and-white pen drawing that has its roots in English illustration, particularly Charles Keene, whose work he admired deeply in spite of its differences in imagery and purpose. In this way, although the book was conceived for private use, it was actually based on mass circulation imagery as if, someday, it would be widely distributed. Sadly, that has never happened. After a *livre de luxe* facsimile produced by Skira in the 1950s, it has been more widely accessible in a smaller French paperback edition, and all its illustrations (without text) have been published in my own book, *Pissarro's People*. In spite of this, it remains on the periphery of impressionist studies, where it is treated as an oddity rather than as *the* central work of anarchist art produced by anyone in the nineteenth century – which is what it actually is.[9]

The work Pissarro created over the last two decades of his life was produced either in or around his barn-studio in the

Fig. 29
Camille Pissarro
Washerwoman, Study, 1880
Oil on canvas, 73 × 59.1 cm
The Metropolitan Museum of Art,
New York. Gift of Mr. and Mrs. Nate
B. Spingold, 1956, 56.184.1

Fig. 30
Camille Pissarro
Illustrations for *Turpitudes Sociales*, 1889–90:
1. *The Temple of the Golden Calf* (plate 3)
2. *Slaves at their Meal* (plate 8)
3. *Art in Stagnation* (plate 17)
4. *Insurrection* (plate 28)
Pen and brown ink over graphite
drawings pasted in an album, 310 × 240 mm
Jean Bonna Collection, Geneva

village of Eragny, north of Paris, or in the many rented hotel suites and apartments he used to make his cityscapes. These are seasonal landscapes painted either from the windows of his studio in inclement weather or from the gardens and fields surrounding his house in good weather. A persistent and painful eye condition forced the elderly painter to work indoors except in warm, windless weather. The landscape paintings have a fidelity to the actual character of the scenery that is rooted in his impressionist practice. The figure paintings are another matter, borrowing from the idealization we have seen operating in his 1882 harvest painting. The two works selected for illustration here, *Apple Picking at Eragny-sur-Epte* of 1888 [fig. 31], in the Dallas Museum of Art, and *Haymakers Resting* of 1891 [fig. 32], in the McNay Museum in San Antonio, Texas, make clear that Pissarro depicted an imagined rural paradise, in which work is collective and fulfilling and where there is something almost unknown in the tradition of French peasant painting that starts with Millet – leisure.[10] If Caillebotte's and Renoir's urban figures play cards, read books, go to the theater, stare out of windows, stroll down the street, rest in the sun, or "pose" for their painter – virtually always at leisure, Pissarro's rural workers work *and* rest, leading lives in which their bodies are strong as a result of their work and their minds are lively, fruit of their leisure.

It is perhaps best to end this brief examination of Pissarro's oeuvre in terms of his anarchist philosophy with a pair of commissioned family photographs, dating from about 1886 and 1890 respectively, still in the hands of the members of the Pissarro family.[11] They tell us everything about the painter's aims as an artist. For the first [fig. 33], the family asked a professional photographer to come to their farm on a nice summer day, when Lucien, who lived in London, was at home, and when Eugénie (Nini) Estruc, the niece of Pissarro's wife, was visiting for the summer. Although almost everyone is simply attired in clothes appropriate for a festive occasion (in place of work), rather than arranged on a terrace or in front of Pissarro's ample and utterly bourgeois house they decided (*he* decided?) to pose on a small haystack in the garden, used for the family animals. We see the Pissarros' five boys (Lucien, Georges, Félix, Ludovic-Rodolphe, and Paul Emile) and their only daughter, Jeanne, with her doll, both parents, one relative, and a young maid, who forms part of the group as one more member of the family, arranged in their garden-farm in a kind

Fig. 31
Camille Pissarro
Apple Picking at Eragny-sur-Epte, 1888
Oil on canvas, 61 × 74 cm
Dallas Museum of Art,
Munger Fund, 1955.17.M

Fig. 32
Camille Pissarro
Haymakers Resting, 1891
Oil on canvas, 65.4 × 81.3 cm
McNay Art Museum, San Antonio,
1950.115

Fig. 33
Pissarro surrounded by his family, Eragny, *c.* 1886
Top, standing, Georges and Félix; center, sitting,
Lucien and Ludovic-Rodolphe; and bottom,
sitting, the maid Juliette (?), Camille, Julie,
Paul-Emile, Jeanne, and Eugenie Estruc.
Archives L&S Pissarro Collection, Paris, inv. P26

of parody of a pyramidal pose from academic art (Camille spoofs in this manner by turning his head so that his gaze and the angle of his jaunty hat create a visual interaction with his son's Lucien and Ludovic-Rodolphe seated in the center). All of this seems utterly delightful and, in a way, ordinary, until we reel back in our memory bank to all the other posed family photographs we have seen from the last decades of the nineteenth century, which were made in studios, with props, stiff-poses, elegant clothes, and a kind of formality that almost everything in the Pissarro family photograph belies. Here is a family without hierarchy (the parents are neither central nor on top) and with a delightful informality and humor that makes them endearing – a family in the country (they had no city property) whose members are each individuals with their own clothing, pose, and character.

The second shot [fig. 34], made half a decade later and slightly more conventional in pose and more organized, is also arranged "on the hay." This time it includes Camille's niece, Alice Isaacson, and his grandson, Tommy, as well as the children who happened to be at home, again the maid, and the family dog. In this case, we simply cannot tell the difference in class and status between the maid, who sits at the far right in front of Pissarro's wife, and the daughter, Jeanne, who sits in front of her father. Their clothing is virtually identical, and each is connected via pose and location with one of the parents. One imagines them springing up after the photograph was made and sitting down to an ample lunch made with produce from the garden, a chicken or fresh ham, and a desert made from fresh fruit and cream and butter or even fresh cheese from their cow. Their collective meal would be little different from the single meal Camille Pissarro had painted more than twenty years before – honest, simple, clean, and made at home. Pissarro's "family of equals" was a supremely anarchist family, and his art was an evocation of a world seen by an artist steeped in anarchist philosophy.

Fig. 34
Pissarro and several members of his family,
Eragny, *c.* 1890
From left to right: Paul-Emile, Jeanne,
Camille, Tommy, Ludovic-Rodolphe,
Alice Isaacson, Julie, and a maid.
Archives L&S Pissarro Collection, Paris, inv. P26

1. *Correspondance de Camille Pissarro*, ed. Janine Bailly-Herzberg, 5 vols. [vol. 1: 1865–85; vol. 2: 1886–90; vol. 3: 1891–94; vol. 4: 1895–98; and vol. 5: 1899–1903] (Saint-Ouen-l'Aumône: Valhermeil, 1986–91), vol. 3, p. 63. "I firmly believe that something of our ideas, born as they are of the anarchist philosophy, passes into our works which are thus antipathetic to the current trend." English translation from Camille Pissarro, *Letters to his Son Lucien*, ed. John Rewald, trans. Lionel Abel (New York: Pantheon, 2nd ed., 1943), p. 163 (henceforward referred to as *Letters to his Son*).

2. See Joachim Pissarro and Claire Durand-Ruel Snollaerts, *Pissarro: Critical Catalogue of Paintings*, 3 vols. (Milan: Skira; Paris: Wildenstein Institute, 2005), vol. 3, pp. 568–71, nos. 868 and 869 (henceforward referred to as *Pissarro: Critical Catalogue*).

3. See Richard Brettell, *Pissarro's People* [exh. cat. Clark Art Institute, Williamstown] (Munich: Prestel; New York: Delmonico Books, 2011), particularly, pp. 35–68, 257–68, and 296–99 (henceforward referred to as *Pissarro's People*).

4. See *Pissarro: Critical Catalogue*, vol. II, pp. 94–95, no. 105.

5. It represents a row of attached houses on a small street parallel to the Route de Versailles that he painted other times, e.g. PDR 135, 137, 160, etc., and the church tower, mistakenly identified as that of Bougival, is clearly the rather squat Louveciennes church tower clearly seen in PDR 160.

6. *Pissarro: Critical Catalogue*, vol. I, p. 126.

7. For a full discussion of these pictures, see Richard Brettell, *Pissarro and Pontoise: The Painter in a Landscape* (New Haven and London: Yale University Press, 1990. French edition, Paris: Valhermeil, 1991), pp. 73–91.

8. For an extended discussion of this painting, see *Pissarro's People*, pp. 157–63.

9. See *Pissarro's People*, pp. 241–55. Also for references to the other editions.

10. See *Pissarro: Critical Catalogue*, vol. III, pp. 555–56, no. 850, and pp. 605–6, no. 920.

11. See *Pissarro's People*, p. 82.

Pissarro

Note to the catalogue

This section of the catalogue includes works on display in both exhibition venues. When a work is only shown in one of these venues, i.e. in Madrid or Barcelona, the symbol [M] or [B], respectively, appears at the end of the entry.

1

Self-Portrait, 1903

Oil on canvas, 41 × 33 cm
Tate: Presented by Lucien Pissarro, the artist's son, 1931
[PDR 1528]

2

The Artist's Palette with a Landscape, c. 1878

Oil on panel, 24.1 × 34.6 cm
Sterling and Francine Clark Art Institute,
Williamstown, Massachusetts
[PDR 562]

I

On the Road to Impressionism

Banks of the Oise at Pontoise, 1867
[cat. 6 detail]

3

La Varenne-Saint-Hilaire, View from Champigny, c. 1863

Oil on canvas, 49.6 × 74 cm
Szépmüvészeti Múzeum, Budapest
[PDR 74]
[M]

4

Banks of the Marne, 1864

Oil on canvas, 81.9 × 107.9 cm
Lent by Glasgow Life (Glasgow Museums) on behalf of Glasgow
City Council. Presented by the Trustees of the Hamilton Bequest, 1951
[PDR 90]

5

The House of Père Gallien, Pontoise, 1866

Oil on canvas, 40.3 × 55.2 cm
Colchester and Ipswich Museum Service
[PDR 111]

6

Banks of the Oise at Pontoise, 1867

Oil on canvas, 45.7 × 71.1 cm
Denver Art Museum, Gift of the Barnett and Annalee Newman
Foundation in honor of Annalee G. Newman, 2001.310
[PDR 117]
[M]

II

Louveciennes - London - Louveciennes 1869–72

7

Louveciennes, 1870

Oil on canvas, 45.8 × 55.7 cm
Southampton City Art Gallery
[PDR 164]

8

Route de Versailles, Louveciennes, Winter Sun and Snow, c. 1870

Oil on canvas, 46 × 55.3 cm
Carmen Thyssen-Bornemisza Collection, on loan
at the Museo Thyssen-Bornemisza, Madrid
[PDR 140]

9

Road to Marly, c. 1870

Oil on canvas, 38.1 × 46 cm
High Museum of Art, Atlanta, Georgia; Purchase with High Museum of Art
Enhancement Fund, funds from the Livingston Foundation, Hambrick Bequest,
Alfred Austell Thornton in memory of Leila Austell Thornton and Albert Edward
Thornton, Sr., and Sarah Miller Venable and William Hoyt Venable, the Phoenix
Society, Mr. and Mrs. Jerome Dobson and Joan N. Whitcomb
[PDR 178]

10

Near Sydenham Hill, 1871

Oil on canvas, 43.5 × 53.5 cm
Kimbell Art Museum, Fort Worth, Texas
[PDR 190]
[M]

11

Dulwich College, c. 1871

Oil on canvas, 49 × 60 cm
Fondation Bemberg, Toulouse, France
[PDR 191]

12

Rue des Voisins, 1871

Oil on canvas, 46 × 55.5 cm
Manchester City Galleries
[PDR 208]

13

The Woods at Marly, 1871

Oil on canvas, 45 × 55 cm
Museo Thyssen-Bornemisza, Madrid
[PDR 210]

14

Chemin des Creux, Louvecienes, Snow, 1872

Oil on canvas, 46 × 55 cm
Museum Folkwang, Essen
[PDR 219]
[M]

III

Pontoise Revisited 1872–82

*The Côte des Boeufs
at L'Hermitage,* 1877
[cat. 23 detail]

15

The Cabbage Field, Pontoise, 1873

Oil on canvas, 60 × 80 cm
Carmen Thyssen-Bornemisza Collection, on loan
at the Museo Thyssen-Bornemisza, Madrid
[PDR 294]

16

Ruelle des Poulies at Pontoise, c. 1872

Oil on canvas, 51.5 × 81.5 cm
Memphis Brooks Museum of Art, Memphis, Tennessee;
Gift of Mr. and Mrs. Hugo N. Dixon, 53
[PDR 264]

17

Road to Ennery, 1874

Oil on canvas, 55 × 92 cm
Musée d'Orsay, Paris, Gift of Max
and Rosy Kaganovitch, 1973
[PDR 349]

18

The Climb, Rue de la Côte-du-Jalet, Pontoise, 1875

Oil on canvas, 54 × 65.7 cm
Brooklyn Museum of Art, Purchased with funds given
by Dikran G. Kelekian (22.60)
[PDR 405]

19

Landscape at L'Hermitage, Pontoise, 1875

Oil on canvas, 54 × 65 cm
Museo Cantonale d'Arte, Lugano
[PDR 400]

20

L'Hermitage at Pontoise, c. 1875–76

Oil on canvas, 49 × 65 cm
Museum Folkwang, Essen
[PDR 332]
[M]

21

Orchard at L'Hermitage, Pontoise, 1877

Oil on canvas, 46 × 55 cm
Musée des beaux-arts, La Chaux-de-Fonds /
Collection René et Madeleine Junod
[PDR 519]

22

A Corner of L'Hermitage, Pontoise, 1878

Oil on canvas, 54.6 × 65 cm
Kunstmuseum Basel
[PDR 553]

23

The Côte des Boeufs at L'Hermitage, 1877

Oil on canvas, 114.9 × 87.6 cm
The National Gallery, London. Presented by C. S. Carstairs
to the Tate Gallery through The Art Fund, 1926; transferred, 1950
[PDR 488]

24

The Pond at Montfoucault, 1875

Oil on canvas, 73.6 × 92.7 cm
The Trustees of the Barber Institute of Fine Arts,
University of Birmingham
[PDR 428]

25

Farm at Montfoucault, 1874

Oil on canvas, 54.5 × 65.5 cm
Collection Albright-Knox Art Gallery, Buffalo, New York,
Bequest of Miss Gertrude Watson, 1938, 1938:16
[PDR 375]

26

The Oise near Pontoise in Gray Weather, 1876

Oil on canvas, 53.5 × 64 cm
Museum Boijmans Van Beuningen, Rotterdam
[PDR 453]
[M]

27

On the Banks of the Oise, Pontoise, 1877

Oil on canvas, 38.5 × 55.6 cm
Williams College Museum of Art, Williamstown, Massachusetts,
Bequest of Governor and Mrs. Herbert H. Lehman, Class of 1899, 77.8.7
[PDR 510]

28

View of Saint-Ouen-l'Aumône, 1876

Oil on canvas, 58.4 × 80.6 cm
Yale University Art Gallery, Gift of Helen G. Altschul,
widow of Frank Altschul, B.A. 1908
[PDR 441]

29

The Path to Le Chou, 1878

Oil on canvas, 57 × 92 cm

Musée de la Chartreuse, Douai

[PDR 542]

30

The Old Road to Ennery at Pontoise, 1877

Oil on canvas, 91.8 × 150 cm
National Gallery of Canada, Ottawa, Gift
of Nahum and Sheila Gelber, Montreal, 1997
[PDR 524]

31

The Quarry at L'Hermitage, Pontoise, 1878

Oil on canvas, 55.7 × 46 cm

Pérez Simón Collection, Mexico

[PDR 576]

[B]

32

Landscape near Pontoise, 1878

Oil on canvas, 54 × 65.1 cm
Columbus Museum of Art, Ohio, Gift of Howard D. and Babette L. Sirak,
the Donors to the Campaign for Enduring Excellence, and the Derby Fund
[PDR 568]
[M]

33

Resting in the Woods, Pontoise, 1878

Oil on canvas, 65 × 54 cm
Hamburger Kunsthalle
[PDR 573]

34

Landscape near Pontoise, 1877

Oil on canvas, 60 × 74 cm
Galleria d'arte moderna di Palazzo Pitti, Soprintendenza Speciale per il Patrimonio
Storico Artistico ed Etnoantropologico e per il Polo Museale della città di Firenze
[PDR 517]
[M]

35

The Farm, 1879

Oil on canvas, 54.6 × 64.8 cm
Collection of the Muskegon Museum of Art,
Gift of the L. C. and Margaret Walker Foundation
[PDR 613]

36

In a Kitchen Garden, 1878

Oil on canvas, 47 × 56 cm
Galleria d'arte moderna di Palazzo Pitti, Soprintendenza Speciale per il Patrimonio
Storico Artistico ed Etnoantropologico e per il Polo Museale della città di Firenze
[PDR 558]
[M]

37

Sente de la Ravinière, Osny, 1883

Oil on canvas, 55.6 × 46.2 cm
Musée des Beaux-Arts, Valenciennes
[PDR 700]

38

Portrait of the Artist's Daughter, 1872

Oil on canvas, 72.7 × 59.5 cm
Yale University Art Gallery, John Hay Whitney,
B.A. 1926, M.A. (Hon.) 1956, Collection
[PDR 281]

39

*Mme Pissarro Sewing
beside a Window*, c. 1877

Oil on canvas, 54 × 45 cm
The Ashmolean Museum, Oxford,
Pissarro Family Gift, 1951
[PDR 534]

40

The Little Country Maid, 1882

Oil on canvas, 63.5 × 53 cm

Tate: Bequeathed by Lucien Pisarro, the artist's son, 1944

[PDR 681]

41

The Maidservant, 1875

Oil on canvas, 92.7 × 73 cm
The Chrysler Museum, Norfolk, Virginia,
Gift of Walter P. Chrysler Jr.
[PDR 418]

42

Roses of Nice, 1902

Oil on canvas, 55 × 47.7 cm
Private collection, Madrid
[PDR 1426]
[B]

43

Still Life with Peonies and Mock Orange, c. 1877

Oil on canvas, 81 × 64 cm
Van Gogh Museum, Amsterdam
(Gift of Sara Lee Corporation)
[PDR 556]

IV

Eragny Landscapes 1884–1903

44

The Haymaker, 1884

Oil on canvas, 73.5 × 60 cm
Pérez Simón Collection, Mexico
[PDR 766]

45

The DelaFolie House, Eragny, Sunset, 1885

Oil on canvas, 73 × 60.5 cm
Musée d'Orsay, Bequest of Clément and Andrée Adès, 1979
(on loan at the Musée de Grenoble)
[PDR 800]

46

View of Bazincourt, 1884

Oil on canvas, 54.3 × 64.8 cm
Pérez Simón Collection, Mexico
[PDR 756]

47

The Village of Eragny, 1885

Oil on canvas, 59.7 × 73 cm
Birmingham Museum of Art, Birmingham (Alabama), Museum purchase
with funds provided by the 1980 Museum Dinner and Ball
[PDR 790]

48

The Field and the Great Walnut Tree in Winter, Eragny, 1885

Oil on canvas, 60 × 73.3 cm
Philadelphia Museum of Art: Purchased
with the W. P. Wilstach Fund, 1921
[PDR 815]

49

The Meadows at Eragny, Apple Tree, 1894

Oil on canvas, 27.3 × 35.6 cm
Carmen Thyssen-Bornemisza Collection, on loan
at the Museo Thyssen-Bornemisza, Madrid
[PDR 1026]

50

Apple Trees at Eragny, Autumn, 1892

Oil on canvas, 55 × 46 cm
Von der Heydt-Museum, Wuppertal
[PDR 962]

51

In the Meadow at Eragny, 1893

Oil on canvas, 46 × 55 cm
Musée d'art et d'histoire, Neuchâtel, Switzerland
Bequest of Yvan and Hélène Amez-Droz
[PDR 1000]

52

The Orchard at Eragny, 1896

Oil on canvas, 54.3 × 65 cm
Carmen Thyssen-Bornemisza Collection,
on loan at the Museo Thyssen-Bornemisza, Madrid
[PDR 1134]

53

Apple Trees and Poplars, Eragny, Sunset, 1901

Oil on canvas, 65 × 81 cm
Musée d'Art moderne André Malraux, Le Havre
[PDR 1395]

54

A Corner of the Meadow at Eragny, 1902

Oil on canvas, 60 × 81.3 cm
Tate: Presented by Mrs. Esther Pissarro, the artist's daughter-in-law, 1951
[PDR 1462]

55

Vegetable Garden, Overcast Morning, Eragny, 1901

Oil on canvas, 64.8 × 81.3 cm

Philadelphia Museum of Art: Bequest of Charlotte Dorrance Wright, 1978

[PDR 1373]

56

Landscape at Varengeville, Gray Weather, 1899

Oil on canvas, 64.8 × 48.9 cm
Collection of Phoenix Art Museum,
Gift of Mr. and Mrs. Donald D. Harrington
[PDR 1288]

57

Landscape at Varengeville, c. 1899

Oil on canvas, 64.8 × 54 cm
Pérez Simón Collection, Mexico
[PDR 1292]

V

City Views

58

On the Bank of the Seine, Paris, The Pont-Marie, Quai d'Anjou, c. 1875

Oil on canvas, 49.5 × 63.5 cm

Pérez Simón Collection, Mexico

[PDR 406]

[B]

59

The Outer Boulevards, Effect of Snow, 1879

Oil on canvas, 54 × 65 cm
Musée Marmottan Monet, Paris
[PDR 618]
[M]

60

L'Île Lacroix, Rouen (The Effect of Fog), 1888

Oil on canvas, 46.7 × 55.9 cm
Philadelphia Museum of Art: John G. Johnson Collection, 1917
[PDR 855]

61

Charing Cross Bridge, London, 1890

Oil on canvas, 60 × 92.4 cm
National Gallery of Art, Washington D.C., Collection
of Mr. and Mrs. Paul Mellon, 1985.64.32
[PDR 884]

62

The Place du Havre, Paris, 1893

Oil on canvas, 60.1 × 73.5 cm
The Art Institute of Chicago, Potter Palmer Collection
[PDR 986]

63

Boulevard Montmartre, Mardi Gras, 1897

Oil on canvas, 65.1 × 81.3 cm
Hammer Museum, Los Angeles, The Armand Hammer Collection,
Gift of the Armand Hammer Foundation
[PDR 1163]
[M]

64

The Boulevard Montmartre on a Winter Morning, 1897

Oil on canvas, 64.8 × 81.3 cm
Lent by The Metropolitan Museum of Art, Gift of Katrin S. Vietor,
in loving memory of Ernest G. Vietor, 1960 (60.174)
[PDR 1160]

65

Morning Sun in the Rue Saint-Honoré,
Place du Théâtre Français, 1898

Oil on canvas, 65.5 × 54 cm
Ordrupgaard, Copenhagen
[PDR 1200]
[M]

66

*Rue Saint-Honoré in the Afternoon,
Effect of Rain*, 1897

Oil on canvas, 81 × 65 cm
Museo Thyssen-Bornemisza, Madrid
[PDR 1196]

67

Garden of the Tuileries in Winter, 1900

Oil on canvas, 66 × 91.4 cm
New Orleans Museum of Art: The Mrs. Frederick
M. Stafford Collection, EL. 1977.12
[PDR 1314]

68

The Tuileries Gardens, 1900

Oil on canvas, 73.6 × 92.3 cm
Lent by Glasgow Life (Glasgow Museums) on behalf
of Glasgow City Council. Presented by Sir John Richmond, 1948
[PDR 1310]
[M]

69

The Louvre, Afternoon, Rainy Weather, 1900

Oil on canvas, 66.5 × 81.5 cm
Corcoran Gallery of Art, Washington D.C.,
Edward C. and Mary Walker Collection
[PDR 1346]

70

The Louvre, Spring, 1901

Oil on canvas, 54 × 65 cm
BAL-Musée des Beaux-Arts de Liège
[PDR 1363]

71

Pont Neuf, Snow Effect, 1902

Oil on canvas, 54.5 × 65.3 cm
National Museum Wales
[PDR 1411]

72

The Pont-Neuf, 1902

Oil on canvas, 55 × 46.5 cm
Szépművészeti Múzeum, Budapest
[PDR 1415]
[M]

73

The Village of Knokke, 1894

Oil on canvas, 54.5 × 65.5 cm
Petit Palais, Musée des Beaux-Arts de la Ville de Paris
[PDR 1036]

74

Pont de la Clef in Bruges, Belgium, 1894–1903

Oil on canvas, 46.4 × 55.2 cm
Manchester City Galleries
[PDR 1034]

75

Bath Road, London, c. 1897

Oil on canvas, 54 × 65 cm
The Ashmolean Museum, Oxford,
Pissarro Family Gift, 1952
[PDR 1182]

76

Fair on a Sunny Afternoon, Dieppe, 1901

Oil on canvas, 73.5 × 92.1 cm
Philadelphia Museum of Art: Bequest
of Lisa Norris Elkins, 1950
[PDR 1388]

77

The Stone Bridge and Barges at Rouen, 1883

Oil on canvas, 54.3 × 65.1 cm
Columbus Museum of Art, Ohio, Gift of Howard D. and Babette L. Sirak,
the Donors to the Campaign for Enduring Excellence, and the Derby Fund
[PDR 728]

78

The Pont Boieldieu and the Pont Corneille, Rouen,
Effect of Rain, 1896

Oil on canvas, 73 × 92 cm
Staatliche Kunsthalle, Karlsruhe
[PDR 1139]

79

The Stone Bridge in Rouen, Dull Weather, 1896

Oil on canvas, 66.1 × 91.5 cm
National Gallery of Canada, Ottawa, Purchased 1923
[PDR 1124]
[M]

80

Pont Boieldieu, Rouen, Effect of Fog, 1898

Oil on canvas, 65.4 × 81.3 cm
Pérez Simón Collection, Mexico
[PDR 1225]

81

View of the Oissel Cotton Mill,
near Rouen, 1898

Oil on canvas, 65.3 × 81 cm
The Montreal Museum of Fine Arts,
Purchase, John W. Tempest Fund
[PDR 1233]

82

The Pilots' Jetty, Le Havre, Morning,
Cloudy and Misty Weather, 1903

Oil on canvas, 65.1 × 81.3 cm
Tate: Presented by Lucien Pissarro, the artist's son, 1948
[PDR 1517]

Paula Luengo

Chronology

1830

Camille Pissarro (named Jacob Abraham Pizarro [sic] on his birth certificate) is born on July 10 in the port of Charlotte Amalie on the island of Saint Thomas, a Danish dependency now part of the US Virgin Islands. He is the third of four children born to Frédéric Pissarro and the Creole Rachel Manzana-Pomié, of French Jewish descent. Rachel was the widow of Isaac Petit and had two daughters from her previous marriage, Delphine and Emma. Upon the death of Isaac, his nephew Frédéric, originally from Portugal, traveled from Bordeaux to Charlotte Amalie to assist Rachel in managing her deceased husband's business. The two married in 1826. Camille's own nationality is Danish, and growing up he learns to speak three languages: French, Spanish and English.

1842

When he turns twelve, Camille is sent to study at the Savary Academy, a French boarding school in Passy, near Paris, where he lives for the following five years. The director of the school, landscape painter and drawing teacher Auguste Savary, discovers and encourages Camille's gift for draftsmanship. His father's family looks after the young man during the holidays. Interested in art from an early age, Pissarro visits the Louvre, the Salons and Savary's studio.

1847

In the summer, Camille returns to Saint Thomas, where he works for his brother Alfred in the family business as a cargo clerk at the docks.

1850

In Charlotte Amalie, Pissarro meets the Danish painter Fritz Melbye, who visits tropical countries to paint exotic landscapes on location for a European clientele. They travel together to Haiti and the Dominican Republic.

1852

Melbye persuades Pissarro to accompany him to Venezuela. They arrive in Caracas on November 12. This voyage proves decisive for Pissarro, for it convinces him to take on painting as a full time profession.

1853

In August, Camille receives a letter from Alfred informing him of the death of his younger brother, Gustave.

1854

Pissarro returns to Saint Thomas after arriving at an agreement with his father: Camille will assume Alfred's duties in the business while his elder brother travels to Paris for five months, but upon his brother's return, Camille will move to Paris to pursue his studies as a painter.

1855

In September, Alfred returns to Saint Thomas and Camille leaves for France on the same boat. The young man arrives in Paris in time to visit the Exposition Universelle and Courbet's Pavilion of Realism, and he is much impressed by the works of Corot and Delacroix. In October, his half-sister, Delphine, dies.

1856

Pissarro attends private classes under various masters from the École des Beaux-Arts without remaining with any one in particular for any length of time. He lives with his family in La Muette and briefly shares a studio with Anton Melbye, Fritz's brother. Fritz arrives in Paris in September.

1857

Dissatisfied with his teachers, Camille enrolls in the Académie Suisse, where he takes life-drawing classes. He meets Corot, from whom he receives informal instruction along with a small group of students to whom Corot recommends *plein air* painting. Pissarro goes on various excursions to the outskirts of Paris. In August he travels to La Roche-Guyon.

1859

In April, the Salon opens in the Palais des Champs-Elysées. The jury accepts one of Pissarro's paintings for the exhibition and mentions him as a student of Anton Melbye in the program. Pissarro's parents are cheered by this first official recognition. During the early years of his artistic career, Pissarro signed his paintings as it appears in his birth certificate, "Pizarro," but beginning in 1859 he returns to the original French spelling of his surname.

1860

Over the previous years, the Pissarro family had gradually moved to France. In his parents' home, Julie Vellay, a twenty-one-year-old Catholic woman from Burgundy, is hired as a kitchen maid. She will become Pissarro's life companion. This year Camille also meets his great friend, the painter Ludovic Piette, as well as Armand Guillaumin and Claude Monet.

1861

Pissarro's parents object to Camille's relationship with Julie, as a result of which she leaves their house and finds work as a florist's assistant. In April, Pissarro meets Paul Cézanne at the Académie

Camille Pissarro, *Pissarro and Fritz Melbye's studio*, c. 1854. Watercolor in brown wash, pencil and black ink on paper, 266 × 367 mm. Banco Central de Venezuela, Caracas

The artist dressed as a *gaucho*, c. 1860. Collection Archives L&S Pissarro, Paris, inv. P1

The house of Ludovic Piette at Montfoucault, before 1906. Postcard. Musée Pissarro Archives, Pontoise

Suisse. At the Louvre he is listed among the artists making copies of works at the museum. The following year he shares a studio with the Danish painter David Jacobsen. He executes numerous views of the countryside around Paris.

1863

Monet introduces Pissarro to his colleagues at Gleyre's atelier: Frédéric Bazille, Alfred Sisley and Auguste Renoir. Pissarro produces his first prints. On February 20, Camille and Julie's first child, Lucien, is born. Three of Pissarro's paintings are put on show in the Salon des Refusés, which features works rejected by the jury of the official Salon. Cézanne, accompanied by Emile Zola, visits the studios of several artists, among them Pissarro's. Pissarro joins the Société des Aquafortistes founded by Alfred Cadart and Félix Chevalier, dealers specializing in prints and modern paintings. In the summer, Camille moves to Saint-Maur, on the outskirts of Paris along the banks of the Marne, and later, in the early autumn, he relocates to the nearby village that lends its name to the title of his painting, *La Varenne-Saint-Hilaire, View from Champigny* [cat. 3].

1864

Camille's father falls ill. Two of Pissarro's works are accepted in the Salon, where he is identified as a student of Corot and Anton Melbye. In December, the artist moves to Saint-Maur, where he rents a house.

1865

Two texts by Pierre-Joseph Proudhon, *De la Justice dans la révolution et dans l'église* (On Justice in the Revolution and the Church, 1858) and *Du Principe de l'art et de sa destination sociale* (On the Principles of Art and its Social Function, 1865), will have a profound impact on Pissarro. For Proudhon, the mission of artistic creation is to educate humankind, to reveal social realities and injustices. Pissarro's father dies on January 28, leaving his mother in the care of her two sons. In May, Julie gives birth to their second child, Jeanne-Rachel, nicknamed Minette. The artist's half-sister, Emma, and her husband, Phinéas Isaacson, move to London. In August, Rachel becomes ill and Camille seeks treatment for her from the homeopathic doctor Paul Gachet, with whom Pissarro develops a lasting friendship. Pissarro exhibits two works in the Salon but sells very little, which compels him to pawn some of his possessions and to rely on the allowance he receives from his mother.

1866

Pissarro's financial situation becomes ever more critical and will continue to vex him for many years. Julie contributes to the family's finances by planting a vegetable garden and helping the local farmers with their harvests. In April, Pissarro moves with his family to Pontoise, on the banks of the Oise River. Easily reachable from Paris by train, this town previously attracted artists such as Daubigny, Morisot and Daumier. There, Pissarro paints *The House of Père Gallien, Pontoise* [cat. 5]. The Salon opens in May and includes a work by Pissarro that receives a favorable review from Zola. Pissarro is introduced to Manet. He participates in the artists' gatherings at the Café Guerbois, on Grande rue des Batignolles, and at Bazille's studio, along with Monet, Renoir, Sisley and other painters. In October, he returns to Paris with his family, where they will remain for half of the year, spending the other half in the outskirts of the city.

1867

Pissarro, Monet, Renoir, Sisley, Bazille, Manet and Cézanne are first excluded by the jury of the Salon and later rejected by the Salon des Refusés as well. Courbet urges this group of artists to exhibit their work outside official circles. Following this advice, Monet and his colleagues prepare an exhibition on the sidelines of the Salon, but in the end the project does not materialize.

1868

Between January 20 and 29, Pissarro travels to London following the death of his sister, Emma. Julie serves as godmother at the baptism of Monet's son, Jean. Together with Guillaumin, Pissarro finds work painting store signs and blinds. Daubigny, as a member of the Salon jury, manages to get two works by Pissarro accepted. Zola writes a long, flattering article about the artist.

1869

In the spring, the Pissarro family moves to Louveciennes.

1870

In January, Pissarro and Monet paint several canvases portraying the effects of a large snowfall in Louveciennes, among them *Route de Versailles, Louveciennes, Winter Sun and Snow* [cat. 8]. In May, two of Pissarro's canvases are accepted at the Salon. In September, war between France and Prussia breaks out. Pissarro and his family flee Louveciennes in great haste and seek refuge at Montfoucault, one of the farms owned by the Piette family in Mayenne. Pissarro wants to enlist, but his family is against this idea; in any case, he lacks French citizenship. On October 21, Julie gives birth to their third child, Adèle-Emma, who dies three weeks after being born. In December, together with Camille's mother and Alfred's family, the Pissarros move to London to live with the Isaacsons.

1871

Pissarro quickly adapts to life in London, but Julie finds it more difficult as she speaks no English. Many other artists from France flee to England around the same time. Daubigny introduces Pissarro to the dealer Paul Durand-Ruel, who has rented the German Gallery on New Bond Street. Through Durand-Ruel, Pissarro gets in touch with Monet, with whom he visits museums where they admire works by Turner, Constable and Old Crome. In May, they participate in the International Exhibition at the South Kensington Museum (now the V&A) with two canvases apiece. Pissarro is not entirely satisfied with his sales. *Near Sydenham Hill* [cat. 10] and *Dulwich College* [cat. 11] both date from this period. In June, Camille and Julie marry in Croydon, Surrey. They return to their home in Louveciennes, which had been plundered during the war. M. Ollivon, a municipal councilor, and his wife manage to save some of their furniture and forty or so paintings from among the 1500 that had been on the premises, representing Pissarro's work over the last twenty years. Camille will receive 835 francs in compensation for the losses he suffered as a consequence of the war, far short of the 51,156 francs he claims in damages. In November, Julie gives birth to their fourth child, Georges-Henri.

1872

Pissarro paints in Louveciennes with Sisley, who lives nearby, and he visits Renoir. In March, Durand-Ruel begins to purchase works by Pissarro on a periodic basis, acquiring twenty-two throughout the year. For the first time, Pissarro earns enough to support his family. In August, he becomes the mentor of a small group of friends who go to Pontoise to paint with him: Guillaumin, Piette, Béliard, Oller and Cézanne. During this period he paints *Ruelle des Poulies at Pontoise* [cat. 16].

1873

Pissarro and Cézanne, who lives in Auvers-sur-Oise, frequently paint together in Pontoise and Auvers. Influenced by Pissarro, Cézanne changes his approach to painting, while Pissarro in turn learns from Cézanne. Doctor Gachet, who is also a printmaker, urges Pissarro, Guillaumin and Cézanne to work in this medium. Each signs his works with a symbol, and Pissarro chooses a head of cabbage. Needing a studio in Paris where he can show his work to possible buyers, Pissarro rents his first *pied-à-terre* in Montmartre. His earlier interest in Japanese arts grows thanks to the influence of his friend, the critic Théodore Duret. Together with Monet, Pissarro makes plans for a painters' cooperative society based on the workers' association model, with the aim of exhibiting and selling their work without having first to go through the Salon.

50. PONTOISE — *Panorama de l'Hermitage - Chapelle du Sacré-Cœur*

398 PONTOISE. — *Panorama de l'Ermitage*

Postcards with views of the hamlet
known as the Hermitage, Pontoise.
Musée Pissarro Archives, Pontoise

Julie Vellay and Camille Pissarro.
Musée Pissarro Archives, Pontoise

Camille's brother, Alfred.
Musée Pissarro Archives, Pontoise

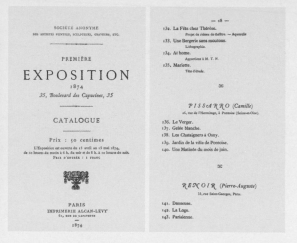

Camille Pissarro and Paul Cézanne (at center)
during one of their *plein air* painting expeditions,
c. 1873. Musée Pissarro Archives, Pontoise

Ludovic Piette, *Camille Pissarro Painting
Outdoors*. Gouache. Private collection

Pissarro, his son Lucien as a boy and
Cézanne, seated on the bench. Musée
Pissarro Archives, Pontoise

Cover and page 18 of the catalogue of the
First Impressionist Exhibition, 1874

1874

In April, Minette dies of a respiratory infection. The family moves to a new house in Pontoise. Two weeks before the Salon opens, the first exhibition of the Société Anonyme des Artistes Peintres, Sculpteurs, Graveurs, etc., opens its doors at the atelier Nadar, on the Boulevard des Capucines. Thirty painters and 167 works appear in the catalogue, including five recent paintings by Pissarro. This First Impressionist Exhibition is a failure. On July 24, Julie gives birth to their fifth child, Félix-Camille, nicknamed Titi, in Pontoise. Pissarro hardly makes any sales and once again feels the pressure of financial difficulties. In October, the family moves to Piette's Montfoucault house, where they will remain until early February of the following year. While there, Pissarro captures his surroundings in works such as *Farm at Montfoucault* [cat. 25].

1876

In April, the Second Impressionist Exhibition is held at the Durand-Ruel gallery. Neither sales nor the opinion of critics and the public improve this time round. The group of impressionists meets for dinner every Wednesday at the house of the collector Eugène Murer. For the third consecutive year, the Pissarros spend the autumn at Montfoucault, where Camille finds numerous subjects to paint and works intensively. To cut down expenses, he gives up his studio in Paris. He also paints ceramics, which sell more readily.

1877

Throughout April, the Third Impressionist Exhibition is held in an apartment located on 6 Rue Le Peletier. It showcases 241 works, twenty-two of which are Pissarro's. The Pissarro family moves to Montfoucault for part of the autumn.

1878

Camille spends long periods in Paris attempting to sell his works. Julie complains of his absences and of the precariousness of their financial situation. On April 15, Pissarro's good friend, Piette, who has been such a major source of assistance, dies of cancer. In May, the Exposition Universelle opens at the Palais du Trocadéro. Caillebotte hopes to take advantage of the large number of visitors to Paris on the occasion by organizing another impressionist exhibition, but his plans come to naught. In November, Julie arrives in Paris with the children and moves into a rented apartment at 18 Rue des Trois-Frères, where they will remain until May 1879. Their sixth child, Ludovic-Rodolphe, named after Ludovic Piette and nicknamed Ludovic-Rodo, is born.

1879

Between April 10 and May 11, the Fourth Impressionist Exhibition takes place in a large apartment on Avenue de l'Opéra. Cézanne, Renoir, Sisley and Morisot are not represented. Only fifteen painters participate, among them Gauguin. Pissarro exhibits thirty-eight works. In Paris he paints canvases such as *The Outer Boulevards, Effect of Snow* [cat. 59]. Julie wants their eldest son, Lucien, who is sixteen, to find work and contribute to the family's finances, but Pissarro objects to this idea, since he wants their son to develop his skills as an artist. In September, Gauguin and Pissarro work together in Pontoise for the first time.

1880

The Fifth Impressionist Exhibition is held, but Cézanne, Renoir, Sisley and Monet, the group's most important members, prefer to participate in the Salon. In order to expand his clientele, Pissarro works in other media: watercolors and prints. Durand-Ruel buys four oils, a gouache and several watercolors from him at the end of December.

1881

Between April 2 and May 1, the Sixth Impressionist Exhibition is held at 35 Boulevard des Capucines. Among the thirteen participants, Raffaëlli and Pissarro contribute the greatest number of works, twenty-eight in the latter's case. In Pontoise, Pissarro receives visits from Cézanne, Gauguin and Guillaumin. Mary Cassatt expresses a desire to rent a house there for the summer but in the event hires one in Louveciennes. On August 27, the Pissarros' seventh child, Jeanne-Marguerite, nicknamed Cocotte, is born.

1882

After Pissarro and Caillebotte manage to reconcile the members of the group, the seventh exhibition of independent artists is held at 251 Rue Saint-Honoré, with the participation of Monet, Sisley, Caillebotte and Renoir. Twenty-six works by Pissarro are presented, and the artist is satisfied with the results. In December, the family moves from Pontoise to Osny.

1883

In February, Camille sends his son Lucien to England to live with his uncle Phinéas Isaacson so that he can avoid military service. In May, upon becoming the artist's sole dealer with exclusive rights to his works, Durand-Ruel organizes Pissarro's first individual exhibition. It features seventy pieces. In the summer, the artist gives up his studio in Paris in order to save money. Shortly thereafter, Pissarro moves to Rouen in search of new subjects. During the months of

October and November he paints thirteen works, among them *The Stone Bridge and Barges at Rouen* [cat. 77]. Monet, Gauguin, Julie and his daughter Jeanne visit him there.

1884

In February, Pissarro rents a house in Eragny, two hours from Paris, a place that will become an important source of inspiration for the artist. Meanwhile, he finds himself obliged to sell his canvases at very low prices in order to make ends meet; he also executes numerous watercolors for small dealers. Julie, at the age of forty-six, gives birth to their eighth and last child, Paul-Emile, in August. Pissarro is a habitual reader of the socialist paper *Le Prolétaire*, as well as of the works of Proudhon, Zola, Flaubert and Kropotkin.

1885

In April, Zola sends Pissarro his novel *Germinal*. In June, Durand-Ruel introduces Pissarro to Octave Mirbeau, a young writer who will become one of the painter's greatest champions in the 1890s. Around the end of August, Pissarro meets up with Cézanne before the latter retires to the south of France. They will not see each other again until Cézanne's great retrospective exhibition at the Vollard gallery in 1895. In the autumn, a few months before meeting the young Paul Signac in Guillaumin's studio, Pissarro and Georges Seurat happen to meet at Durand-Ruel's gallery. As a result of these encounters and given that Pissarro has begun to harbor doubts about his own art at the time, he begins to experiment with a new technique, pointillism. He adopts the ideals of anarchism and reads Jean Grave's paper, *Le Révolté*.

1886

Pissarro remains in Paris throughout most of the month of January, attempting to sell his work, while Julie reproaches him for their difficult economic situation, fruit of the painter's increasing debts. Since Durand-Ruel has likewise (and for some time) been encountering financial difficulties, Pissarro decides to entrust other dealers with the sale of his works. He continues to paint in a pointillist style, despite the fact that almost all critics reject this technique. During the months of May and June, the Eighth Impressionist Exhibition is held, in which Signac, Seurat, Pissarro and his son, Lucien, show their works in a separate room. Monet, Renoir, Sisley and Caillebotte do not participate in the show, which presents a very heterogeneous group of artists. Pissarro meets Vincent van Gogh, recently installed in Paris.

1887

Pissarro encounters difficulties finding buyers, since few collectors are fond of his new pointillist style, about which even Durand-Ruel is ambivalent. Because of his financial problems, Pissarro must sell a drawing by Degas and a bronze by Barye from his personal collection. In the spring, he becomes friends with the painter Maximilien Luce after admiring one of his works in the Salon des Indépendants. In the autumn, Theo van Gogh, Vincent's brother and an art dealer, begins to sell Pissarro's work.

1888

During this period, Pissarro and Vincent van Gogh attend the same artists' gatherings in Paris. Back in Eragny, Pissarro fears that art dealers will forget him. Nevertheless, in April he manages to sell thirty-one works to Durand-Ruel for 5,000 francs, which temporarily alleviate his financial problems. The dealer's own situation has improved owing to the success of his gallery in New York. Relations between Pissarro and Monet become tense. In July, Pissarro is visited by Luce, with whom he shares an appreciation for neo-impressionism and anarchist ideas. During the month of August, Pissarro's eye problem, which he has been suffering since 1880, worsens, and he develops an infection that interferes with his work. At the same time, he begins to develop serious doubts about neo-impressionism: he is aware that it requires an extremely slow, painstaking kind of work and that it does not sell well. In December, he again rents a small studio in Paris, at 12 Rue de l'Abreuvoir.

1889

On May 30, Pissarro's mother dies at the age of ninety-four. Alfred and his wife seek to leave Camille out of the inheritance. In June, Pissarro's son Georges leaves for London to improve his English, and a frequent correspondence is set up between France and England. Georges enrolls in the Guild and School of Handicraft. Theo van Gogh asks Pissarro to take care of Vincent, who has just left the asylum to which he had committed himself because of his psychological problems. Julie objects to this, so Pissarro recommends Paul Gachet as a doctor equipped to help Vincent during his convalescence.

1890

Pissarro distances himself from neo-impressionism. In January, he sends his nieces in London, Esther and Alice Isaacson, the album of twenty-eight anarchist drawings titled *Turpitudes Sociales* (Social Disgraces) [see fig. 30], dated the previous year, with the aim of providing them with instruction. A month later, Theo van Gogh organizes a show of Pissarro's works at the Boussod et Valadon

Paul Gauguin and Camille Pissarro,
Portraits of One Another, c. 1880.
Charcoal and pastel on paper,
358 × 495 mm. Musée d'Orsay, Paris

Maximilien Luce, *The Pissarro Family:
Paul-Emile, Camille, Félix, Georges and
Ludovic-Rodolphe*, c. 1890. Lithography.
Musée de l'Hôtel-Dieu, Mantes-la-Jolie

gallery, in which only five canvases are sold. In April, Pissarro is obliged to sell a work by Daubigny from his own collection in order to pay off debts. His brother dies in May, following the deterioration of their relationship over the family inheritance. In the early summer, Pissarro, Luce and Lucien visit Georges in London, where they stay with the Isaacsons. Among other things, Pissarro paints views of Hyde Park and Kensington Gardens, as well as *Charing Cross Bridge, London* [cat. 61]. Georges returns home with his father while Lucien settles permanently in London, marking the beginning of a long correspondence between father and son. Lucien attempts to earn a living by teaching drawing, and Camille assists him financially. During this period and together with his sons, Pissarro works in the medium of printmaking. His eye infection recurs. On July 28, Vincent van Gogh dies.

1891

Pissarro's relations with Julie become very tense: she wants her sons to find work with which they can contribute to the family's finances, but their father continues to voice his opposition. On January 21, Theo van Gogh dies, and shortly thereafter, Pissarro makes his works available to the dealer Alphonse Portier. Seurat dies of diphtheria on March 29. In May, Pissarro's eye ailment worsens due to an abscess, and he has surgery in July. As a result, he cannot work for long periods away from home and is forced to paint indoors, looking out from a window. He returns to Eragny. In September, Georges leaves for London to live with Lucien. Mary Cassatt assists Pissarro in the sale of his works to American collectors and also sends him young students for him to teach.

1892

For the first time after many years of hardship, Pissarro no longer has difficulty selling his paintings, and several dealers compete for his work. His retrospective exhibition at the Durand-Ruel gallery is a success. From May 23 to August 13 he resides in London with his two sons. While there, he paints eleven views of Kew and two of London. Back in France, his landlord, M. Dallemagne, puts up the house in Eragny for sale. Julie, wishing to buy it, asks Monet for a loan of 15,000 francs without consulting with her husband. In July, they purchase the house for 31,000 francs (double the original price), and a month later Pissarro visits Monet to thank him for the generous gesture. In August, Lucien marries Esther Bensusan in Richmond, a ceremony at which only his father and brother are present. Esther's family does not attend, thereby expressing their objection to the marriage on the grounds that Lucien is not a practicing Jew. Durand-Ruel insists on being Pissarro's sole dealer, but the artist refuses him exclusivity. Camille's son Georges secretly

The artist around 1890–95. Musée
Pissarro Archives, Pontoise

From left to right, Pissarro and his sons
Ludovic-Rodolphe, Lucien and Félix in
Knokke, 1894. Musée Pissarro Archives,
Pontoise

Pissarro at the window of his studio in
Eragny, palette in hand, *c.* 1891. Musée
Pissarro Archives, Pontoise

Camille Pissarro on the stairs leading to his
studio in Eragny, *c.* 1893. Musée Pissarro
Archives, Pontoise

marries his cousin, Esther Isaacson, fourteen years his elder. During his sojourn in Paris, Pissarro stays at the Hôtel Garnier, 111 Rue Saint-Lazare.

1893

Pissarro travels to and from Paris. Between February 27 and May 15, he falls ill and is compelled to remain in the capital. While there, he works from his hotel room window, painting four views of Rue Saint-Lazare and the Place du Havre, among them *The Place du Havre, Paris* [cat. 62]. Between March 15 and 30, his second one-man show at the Galerie Durand-Ruel features forty-one recent works. He meets Henri de Toulouse-Lautrec. He suffers another eye infection and undergoes another operation. Durand-Ruel requests canvases with figures and Pissarro works on the subject of women bathing. In October, work begins on the remodeling of the granary in the garden of Pissarro's house, with a view to converting it into a studio. In December, Durand-Ruel buys works from Pissarro for 23,600 francs.

1894

Beginning this year, Pissarro renews his interest in lithography and etching, and purchases a press from Auguste Delâtre. He also establishes his first commercial contacts with Ambroise Vollard, initiated when Pissarro exchanges a work of his own for a Manet in Vollard's possession. In March, Durand-Ruel opens the third retrospective of Pissarro's recent work. The painter resides for three and a half months in Belgium with his son Félix to avoid the tense political climate in France following the assassination of President Sadi Carnot by an anarchist. He stays in Knokke-sur-Mer, near his young friend, the painter Théo van Rysselberghe, where Pissarro paints works such as *The Village of Knokke* [cat. 73] and *Pont de la Clef in Bruges, Belgium* [cat. 74].

1895

Once again sales fall and Pissarro begins to worry about his financial situation, for he continues to support his children. In January, Van Rysselberghe and his wife visit the Pissarros in Eragny. On March 5, Berthe Morisot dies. In the month of April, Pissarro stays briefly with the Spanish painter Darío de Regoyos in Rouen. At the end of May, he visits two important exhibitions: Monet's Rouen Cathedral series and the show marking Corot's hundredth birthday.

1896

Between January 20 and March 30, Pissarro settles in Rouen at the Grand Hôtel de Paris, where he rents two rooms, one of which he uses as a studio. From there he paints the port. In the spring,

Durand-Ruel presents thirty-five works by Pissarro, including eleven views of Rouen. The show is a success and thanks to the high number of sales, Pissarro is able to settle his debt with Monet. From September 8 to November 12 he returns to Rouen, where he resides at the Hôtel d'Angleterre, from which he can see the Pont Boieldieu and the Pont Corneille, with the Ile Lacroix and the district of Saint-Sever in the distance. He paints thirteen oils in ten weeks, among them *The Pont Boieldieu and the Pont Corneille, Rouen, Effect of Rain* [cat. 78] and *The Stone Bridge in Rouen, Dull Weather* [cat. 79]. At the end of November, Pissarro sends his sons Félix and Georges (who is ill) to San Sebastián with Darío de Regoyos. From there they travel to Barcelona, returning to Paris in January of the following year.

1897

Durand-Ruel acquires all of the Paris oil cityscapes in Pissarro's possession: six works depicting Rue Saint-Lazare, Rue d'Amsterdam and the Place du Havre. The dealer urges him to return to Paris to execute a new series of views of the capital, this time portraying its main boulevards: *Boulevard Montmartre, Mardi Gras* [cat. 63] and *The Boulevard Montmartre on a Winter Morning* [cat. 64]. Pissarro moves to the Grand Hôtel de Russie, on the corner of Rue Drouot and the Boulevard des Italiens. In April he attends the exhibition of the estate of Gustave Caillebotte at the Musée de Luxembourg, following the artist's death three years earlier. It is the first time that impressionist works are shown in a French museum. Durand-Ruel organizes Pissarro's first American exhibition in his gallery on Fifth Avenue in New York, where he shows forty-two of his works. In mid-March, Pissarro meets Henri Matisse. In May, he travels to London to visit Lucien, who is sick. During his stay there, he executes seven views of Bedford Park from his son's house, including *Bath Road, London* [cat. 75]. The members of the Pissarro family get together in Eragny in the summer. Back in England, Félix is diagnosed with tuberculosis and is admitted to the sanatorium at Blenheim House, in Kew, where he dies on November 25 at the age of twenty-three.

1898

Between January and April, Pissarro moves to the Grand Hôtel du Louvre at 172 Rue de Rivoli, a venue with magnificent views of the Opera and the corner of the Place du Palais Royal. He paints *Morning Sun in the Rue Saint-Honoré, Place du Théâtre Français* [cat. 65] and *Rue Saint-Honoré in the Afternoon, Effect of Rain* [cat. 66]. Of the fifteen views that he makes, Durand-Ruel purchases twelve in May. The Dreyfus affair divides France. Zola publishes "J'accuse!" in the newspaper *L'Aurore*, an open letter to the president of the Republic denouncing the injustice committed against the Jewish officer Alfred Dreyfus, and he flees to London to avoid repression by the government. Among intellectuals, a massive campaign is organized to demand a new trial for Dreyfus. Degas, Renoir and Guillaumin shun Pissarro on account of his support for this cause. Their financial situation having improved, Camille and Julie are able to travel through Burgundy for three weeks in the summer. In July, Pissarro returns to Rouen and stays at the Hôtel d'Angleterre, where he paints twenty new works. Among them are *Pont Boieldieu, Rouen, Effect of Fog* [cat. 80] and *View of the Oissel Cotton Mill, near Rouen* [cat. 81].

1899

Pissarro spends the winter and the early spring with Julie and their children Jeanne and Paul-Emile in Paris. They rent an apartment at 204 Rue de Rivoli, where Pissarro paints beside a window. Of the fourteen views he makes of the Tuileries – among them *Garden of the Tuileries in Winter* [cat. 67] and *The Tuileries Gardens* [cat. 68] – Durand-Ruel buys eleven. On January 29, Alfred Sisley dies. The Bernheim-Jeune gallery exhibits twenty-three works by Pissarro and sells nearly all of them. Durand-Ruel organizes a group exhibition with works by Monet, Renoir, Sisley and thirty-six paintings by Pissarro. In June, the painter returns to the countryside, to Eragny, in search of new subjects. From early September to October 13, Pissarro stays in Varengeville-sur-Mer, to the west of Dieppe, not far from the sea. His family joins him. The seven oil paintings he produces there are landscapes depicting inland areas, such as *Landscape at Varengeville, Gray Weather* [cat. 56] and *Landscape at Varengeville* [cat. 57]. For the third consecutive year, Pissarro participates in the annual exhibition (the fourth) held at the Carnegie Institute in Pittsburgh, Pennsylvania.

1900

Pissarro has for several years generously supported various causes of the anarchist movement (publications and newspapers, *soupes-conférences*, the Université Populaire in Nancy, etc.). Paris once again hosts the Exposition Universelle. At the Centennale – the international exhibition of art held at the Grand Palais des Champs-Elysées – an entire room is devoted to impressionism. Pissarro shows seven oils and a drawing. He spends the summer in Berneval and the fall in Eragny, where he captures the colors and light of the autumnal landscapes. He also works with Lucien creating prints. Having exhausted the possibility for new views of the Tuileries, in November he rents a new apartment in Paris on the Place Dauphine, on the Ile de la Cité, situated on the corner of the Pont

Neuf. During this period he paints *The Louvre, Afternoon, Rainy Weather* [cat. 69] and *The Louvre, Spring* [cat. 70].

1901

On January 14, Durand-Ruel's gallery presents the artist's first individual exhibition since 1898. He shows forty-two recent oil paintings that include views of Rouen and of the Tuileries Gardens, as well as landscapes of Eragny, Varengeville and Berneval. Pissarro manages to get his two principal dealers, Durand-Ruel and Bernheim-Jeune, to compete for his work. This rivalry proves advantageous for the painter, who sees the price of his work climb. During the months of April and May, Pissarro stays with his son Georges in Moret-sur-Loing, where he paints a series of six oils. This is probably where he meets the young Francis Picabia. Pissarro spends the summer in Dieppe. He stays at the Hôtel du Commerce next to the Place Nationale and the statue of Admiral Duquesne, while his family moves into a rented house in nearby Berneval. He produces nine canvases with views of the church of Saint-Jacques and of the market, such as *Fair on a Sunny Afternoon, Dieppe* [cat. 76]. For the third consecutive year, Pissarro spends October in Eragny. During the winter he resides in Paris, working from his apartment. He regularly asks Durand-Ruel, and later Bernheim-Jeune, to send his sons the allowance he himself used to make available to them before then. Pissarro's dealers also settle his accounts with his suppliers.

1902

In February, an exhibition featuring Monet's Vétheuil series and Pissarro's recent work – including five views of Dieppe and eight of Paris – opens in the Bernheim-Jeune gallery. The critics acclaim Pissarro. During the summer, he settles in Dieppe, where he paints twenty-one views of the port. On September 29, Emile Zola dies. Pissarro again spends the early autumn in Eragny and the winter in Paris, where he paints *Pont Neuf, Snow Effect* [cat. 71] and *The Pont-Neuf* [cat. 72]. Neither Durand-Ruel nor Bernheim-Jeune offers to buy his views of Dieppe, having agreed with each other to purchase his work at a lower price. In view of this, Pissarro is obliged to curtail expenses.

1903

Pissarro finally sells his Dieppe canvases to the young dealer Félix Gérard. In search of a new subject, he rents a room for two months at the Hôtel du Quai Voltaire, on the right bank of the Seine, which looks out onto the Louvre. Back in Eragny, he continues to work on his spring series. He also travels for several days to Dieppe to work on his summer series. He spends the summer in Le Havre, at

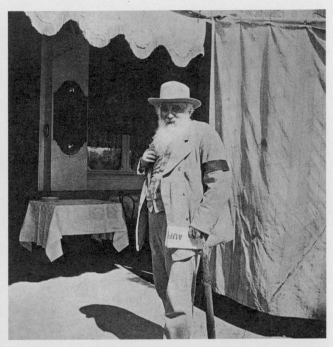

Pissarro in Rouen, in front of the Hôtel d'Anglaterre, holding a copy of the newspaper *L'Aurore* and wearing a mourning bracelet, possibly for the death of his son Félix, 1898. Musée Pissarro Archives, Pontoise

The Avenue de l'Opera in Paris

The artist standing before several of his works (among them, cat. 78) in the apartment on Rue de Rivoli, c. 1900. Musée Pissarro Archives, Pontoise

Pissarro and his portable easel with Julie, Paul-Emile and Jeanne in the orchard at Eragny, c. 1900. Musée Pissarro Archives, Pontoise

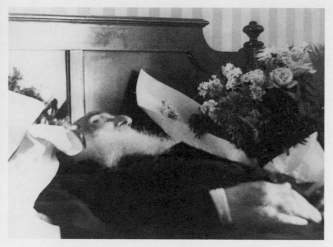

Jeanne, Ludovic-Rodolphe, Julie and Camille in Dieppe, 1901–2. Musée Pissarro Archives, Pontoise

Georges, Ludovic-Rodolphe, Julie, Alice Isaacson with her youngest son Tommy, Camille and Jeanne before the church of Saint-Jacques in Dieppe, 1902. Collection Archives L&S Pissarro, Paris

View of the market in Dieppe

Camille Pissarro on his deathbed, 1903. Musée Pissarro Archives, Pontoise

the Hôtel Continental, where he paints such works as *The Pilots'
Jetty, Le Havre, Morning, Cloudy and Misty Weather* [cat. 82].
The Musée du Havre purchases two views of the city by Pissarro.
It is the first time that a public institution in France acquires work
by the artist (though the previous year he donated a canvas to the
Museum of Fine Arts in Dieppe). In the autumn he resides in Paris,
where he rents two rooms with views onto the Bassin de l'Arsenal.
At this time he executes his fourth and final self-portrait [cat. 1].
On September 29, he participates in the act commemorating
the death of Zola, which consists of a pilgrimage to Médan.
Subsequently, in October he falls ill and has to remain in his room
in the Hôtel Garnier. He is later moved to his apartment. Lucien
travels from London to see his father, whose health continues to
deteriorate steadily. On November 13, surrounded by his family,
Camille Pissarro dies. He is buried in the Père-Lachaise Cemetery
in Paris. Julie Pissarro will live until 1926.

1904
The Durand-Ruel gallery organizes a major retrospective of the
artist in which 130 of Pissarro's works are put on show. Octave
Mirbeau signs the preface to the catalogue.

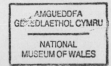

Illustration Credits

Exhibition

Curator
Guillermo Solana

Technical Curator
Paula Luengo

Registrar
Lucia Cassol

Installation, Production and Promotion
Museo Thyssen-Bornemisza

Graphic Design and Signage
Sánchez/Lacasta

This exhibition is largely covered by the
Spanish Government Indemnity Scheme

Catalogue

Published by
Museo Thyssen-Bornemisza

Essays
Richard R. Brettell
Joachim Pissarro
Guillermo Solana

Documentation
Paula Luengo

Editorial Coordination
Museo Thyssen-Bornemisza
Publications Department
Ana Cela
Catali Garrigues
Ángela Villaverde
Carmen Hevia

Copy Editor
Erica Witschey

Translation
Michael Agnew

Graphic Design
Sánchez/Lacasta
Adcla Morán

Layout
Myriam López Consalvi

Prepress
Lucam

Printing
Brizzolis

Binding
Ramos

Cover: Camille Pissarro, *Route de Versailles, Louveciennes,
Winter Sun and Snow*, c. 1870 [detail cat. 8]

© of the edition: Fundación Colección Thyssen-Bornemisza, 2013
© of the texts: their authors
© of the photographs: see illustration credits

ISBN English softcover edition: 978-84-15113-41-6
Legal deposit: M-15334-2013
ISBN English hardcover edition: 978-84-15113-42-3
Legal deposit: M-15625-2013

EXPOSITION
CAMILLE PISSARRO

– 1890 –

This catalogue,
published on the occasion
of the exhibition
Pissarro,
was printed in May 2013